Teaching Physical Education in the Primary School

In order to teach physical education, teachers need additional skills, knowledge and understanding to those required by other subjects in the primary curriculum. *Teaching Physical Education in the Primary School* provides professional development for teachers, and it aims to increase knowledge and understanding, confidence and enthusiasm in an area of the curriculum that often receives a very short time allocation during initial teacher training courses.

The areas covered by *Teaching Physical Education in the Primary School* include:

- subject knowledge of different activity areas: games, gymnastics, dance, swimming, outdoor activities, athletic activities and health-related fitness and exercise;
- safety and organization of children and equipment;
- appropriate teaching points to improve children's skills;
- teachers' self-evaluation;
- adaptation strategies for children with special needs.

Teaching Physical Education in the Primary School will be useful for primary teachers, subject leaders responsible for professional development and trainee teachers. It focuses on giving practical advice to develop teachers' skills to ensure that children are taught effectively and safely in physical education.

Bev Hopper, **Jenny Grey** and **Trish Maude** have extensive experience of teaching physical education in primary schools. They teach on undergraduate and postgraduate initial teacher training courses in physical education and offer a wide range of courses for the continuing professional development of practising primary teachers. They currently lecture in Primary Curriculum and Professional Studies at Homerton College, Cambridge.

Teaching Physical Education in the Primary School

Bev Hopper, Jenny Grey and Trish Maude

ROUTLEDGE · FALMER
Taylor & Francis Group

First published 2000
by RoutledgeFalmer
11 New Fetter Lane, London EC4P 4EE

Simultaneously published in the USA and Canada
by RoutledgeFalmer
29 West 35th Street, New York, NY 10001

RoutledgeFalmer is an imprint of the Taylor & Francis Group

© 2000 Bev Hopper, Jenny Grey and Trish Maude

Typeset in Melior by Taylor & Francis Books Ltd
Printed and bound in Great Britain by TJ International Ltd,
Padstow, Cornwall

British Library Cataloguing in Publication Data
A catalogue record for this book is available from the British Library

Library of Congress Cataloging in Publication Data
Hopper, Bev
    Teaching physical education in the primary school/ Bev Hopper,
    Jenny Grey & Trish Maude.
    p. cm.
    Includes bibliographical references (p.) and index.
    1. Physical education and training–Study and teaching (Elementary)–
    Great Britain. 2. Physical education teachers–Training of–Great Britain.
    I. Grey, Jenny. II. Maude, Patricia. III. Title.

    GV443 .H62 2000   99-087134

ISBN 0–415–23028–4

Contents

Chapter 1
What is Physical Education in the Primary School?   3

Chapter 2
Knowledge and Understanding of the Six Areas of Activity   7

Chapter 3
Physical Education and Other Areas of the Whole Curriculum   91

Chapter 4
Planning for Physical Education at Key Stages 1 and 2 100

Chapter 5
and Management of Physical Education at Key Stages 1 and 2 121

Chapter 6
Assessment, Recording and Reporting in Physical Education 133

Chapter 7
Study Sheets 143

Illustrations

Tables

Figures

Introduction

In order to teach physical education teachers need additional skills, knowledge and understanding to those required by other subjects in the primary curriculum. Teachers are working with active, moving children in a large space and often a large amount of equipment. They need to be able to teach from observation, differentiate a very wide range of activities and of course, there is the continual awareness of risk assessment and concern for safety.

During Initial Teacher Training (ITT) the time allocated to physical education has been reduced due partly to the increased demands of English, mathematics, science and information and communication technology in the timetables of trainee teachers. In school, the mentors of trainee teachers often express their own insecurities about teaching physical education and many feel unable to offer much support.

As college tutors, we searched for a book that we could recommend to primary trainee teachers in order to supplement their short physical education ITT courses. They needed something that offered them knowledge and understanding about the six areas of activity, management, organization, planning, teaching and assessment, appropriate to inexperienced teachers of primary physical education.

Such a book did not seem to exist, so we set about writing our own pack of materials to support our primary ITT physical education college-based courses. Soon class teachers then began to ask if they could buy their own copies; they had seen the trainee teachers' packs and found them useful too. As a result, this book was written.

The 'Study Sheets' in Chapter 7 are useful for professional development in a variety of contexts. Subject leaders may want to use them as a focus for staff meetings. This can be particularly beneficial if teachers have the opportunity to complete some of the sheets whilst observing the subject leader working with a class of children. A great deal of rich discussion is likely to be generated! The sheets are useful for newly qualified teachers who may need to develop their confidence and competence in teaching physical education by watching another teacher teaching physical education as part of their induction process. For trainee teachers the sheets offer foci for observing children being taught either in school or in college and offer a wide range of possibilities for private study.

We have tried to ensure that the book is 'user friendly' and focuses on giving practical advice to develop teachers' skills in order that children learn and are taught effectively and safely in physical education.

Although *Teaching Physical Education in Primary Schools* is written to take into account the recommendations of the QCA document *Maintaining Breadth and Balance* (1998), its practical nature will ensure that the book will be useful no matter what new legislation brings.

Primary teachers who feel their own training in physical education was rather short, subject leaders who are responsible for the professional development of their colleagues and of course, trainee teachers will all find this book helpful.

| Chapter 1 | What is Physical Education in the Primary School? |

Primary physical education teaching has undergone many changes, from the *Syllabus of Physical Training for Schools* (Board of Education, 1933), through *Planning the Programme: Physical Education in the Primary School* (HMSO, 1953) to the *Physical Education in the National Curriculum* (Department for Education, 1995) and now *Maintaining Breadth and Balance at Key Stages 1 and 2* (Qualifications and Curriculum Authority, 1998).

Whilst it is expected that the new millennium will bring revised curriculum orders for all the foundation subjects, those for physical education are not expected to be radically different from the current recommendations of the Qualifications and Curriculum Authority (QCA).

The current recommendations are not new. They have been adapted from the Physical Education in the National Curriculum (DFE, 1995). However, the implementation of the National Literacy Strategy and the proposed National Numeracy Strategy has led to schools being given more flexibility about teaching the National Curriculum in foundation subjects. Schools no longer have to teach the full programmes of study in these subjects as long as they maintain a curriculum that is broad, balanced and relevant to children's needs. Whilst the QCA feels that these arrangements should not involve major re-planning of the Key Stages 1 and 2 curriculum, examples of how curriculum plans might be modified by prioritizing, combining or reducing are given in the document *Maintaining Breadth and Balance* (QCA, 1998).

This QCA document outlines the new flexible arrangements for the National Curriculum in foundation subjects at Key Stages 1 and 2. In physical education, the QCA currently states what physical education is about at each key stage, lists the key aspects, which are important for all children, that should be taught and states the expectations for children's knowledge, understanding and skills by the end of key stage.

What physical education is about at Key Stage 1

At Key Stage 1, children develop physical skills, begin to link them to form short sequences or series of movements and learn to make simple judgements about their performance. They build on their own creativity and enthusiasm for physical activity using indoor and outdoor environments. Children work alone, learn to co-operate and work with a partner. They become aware of the changes that occur to their bodies as they exercise and recognise the short term effects.

Key aspects drawn from the programme of study for Key Stage 1

- Developing a positive attitude to physical activity and health.
- Learning safe practices. In particular, responding readily to instructions and learning how to lift, carry and place equipment safely.
- Actively engaging in the continuous process of planning, performing and evaluating, through dance, games and gymnastic activities, with the greatest emphasis on performance.

Expectations

By the end of Key Stage 1, it is expected that most children will be able to:

In dance

- show control and co-ordination in the basic actions of travelling, jumping, turning, gesturing and stillness;
- perform simple rhythmic patterns and use movement expressively to explore moods and feelings in response to stimuli, including music.

In games

- send, receive, travel with a ball and similar equipment;
- play simple games that involve running, chasing, dodging and avoiding, individually, in pairs and in small groups.

In gymnastic activities

- perform the basic actions of travelling, rolling, jumping, balancing, climbing and swinging using the floor and apparatus;
- link actions together both on the floor and using apparatus.

What physical education is about at Key Stage 2

At Key Stage 2, children develop their skills and become increasingly able to plan, perform and evaluate what they do. Children work co-operatively and competitively in a range of physical activities involving creative tasks, problem solving and decision making. They practise movements and sequences to improve and refine their performance and make judgements about their own and others' work. They sustain energetic activity over appropriate periods of time and understand the short-term effects of exercise.

Key aspects drawn from the programme of study for Key Stage 2

- Developing positive attitudes to physical activity and healthy lifestyles.
- Learning safe practices. In particular, following rules, laws, codes and safety procedures for different activities and knowing how to warm up and recover from exercise.
- Activity engaging in the continuous process of planning, performing and evaluating through a range of activities, including dance, games, gymnastic activities and swimming, and, if possible, athletic activities and outdoor and adventurous activities.

Expectations

By the end of Key Stage 2 it is expected that most children will be able to:

In dance

- compose and combine basic actions by varying shape, size, direction, level, speed, tension and continuity;
- express feelings, moods and ideas through movement in response to stimuli including music;
- perform dances from different times and places.

In games

- send, receive and travel with a ball with increasing control and accuracy;
- play individual and simplified small-sided versions of team games;
- understand and apply the principles of attack and defence.

In gymnastic activities

- perform different ways of jumping, rolling, turning and balancing, travelling on hands and feet, and climbing and swinging emphasising changes of shape, speed and direction;
- plan and perform more complex sequences both on the floor and apparatus.

In athletic activities

- compare and improve their performance and techniques in running, jumping and throwing.

In outdoor and adventurous activities

■ perform activities of a physical and problem-solving nature.

(QCA, 1998)

Whilst the QCA document *Maintaining Breadth and Balance* outlines the new flexible arrangements for the National Curriculum in foundation subjects at Key Stages 1 and 2, there is no flexibility for swimming. The document clearly states that:

■ Swimming remains a statutory requirement.
■ Pupils should be taught the current National Curriculum requirements for swimming unless they have already completed the programme of study during Key Stage 1.
■ If aspects of the swimming programme of study have been taught during Key Stage 1, pupils should be taught the Key Stage 2 swimming programme starting at the appropriate point.

Consequently the expectations for swimming come from the National Curriculum:

National Curriculum for Physical Education: Programme of Study for Swimming in Key Stage 1 and/or 2

Pupils should be taught:
a   to swim unaided, competently and safely, for at least 25 metres;
b   to develop confidence in water, and how to rest, float and adopt support positions;
c   a variety of means of propulsion using either arms or legs or both, and how to develop effective and efficient swimming strokes on the front and the back;
d   the principles and skills of water safety and survival.

(DFE, 1995)

The fact that swimming is the only area of any foundation subject that has remained statutory and for which the full programme of study from the National Curriculum Orders for Physical Education is still to be taught, reflects its importance amongst the other five areas of activity.

Chapter 2 — Knowledge and Understanding of the Six Areas of Activity

Physical education in the primary school is made up of six areas of activity: games, gymnastic activities, dance, swimming, outdoor and adventurous activities and athletic activities. Primary schools currently have flexibility to select from these areas, except for swimming at Key Stage 2, which remains statutory, but they must retain a broad and balanced curriculum.

GAMES

Games is not just about running around on a cold, muddy field! Games can contribute to the development of the whole child, including motor competence, creative thinking, conceptual understanding, problem solving and personal development.

Since the publication of John Major's *Sport: Raising the Game* in 1995 (Department of National Heritage, 1995), schools have been encouraged to give greater emphasis to games in both the curriculum and extra-curricula time and many schools give greater weight to games than to other areas of activity in the physical education curriculum.

At the primary level, teachers are not expected to teach children to play the adult version of recognized games in curriculum time. This would be inappropriate as their level of physical competence and understanding of the principles of each game are not sufficiently developed.

Although some schools choose to work with their most able children in extra-curricular time on the adult versions of some games, the QCA clearly states that children in Key Stages 1 and 2 should be taught games skills as individuals, pairs and in small groups – 'simplified small sided games'.

Categories of Games Skills

Adult games are subdivided into three categories:

Invasion games: where the aim is for one team to invade another team's territory and attack a goal or line, e.g. soccer, rugby, hockey, netball, basketball.

Over-the-net-type games: where the aim is to strike an object across a barrier into an opponent's area so that it cannot be returned, e.g. tennis, volleyball, badminton.

Striking and fielding games: where the aim is for the batting team to strike a ball, which may be delivered by a member of the fielding team, e.g. cricket, rounders, softball, stoolball.

Whilst many games have some common principles, each category has different intentions, makes different demands on players and focuses on different areas of skill. The intentions, demands and skill areas for each games category are listed below.

Invasion Games

Intentions:
- to score by manoeuvring an object through defended territory to an agreed target or targets
- to respond to the ebb and flow of play as determined by possession in a shared playing area
- to have the higher score at the termination of play; game time being determined beforehand.

Demands:
- to understand one's own responsibilities whether in attack or defence
- to move the ball towards the target to create scoring opportunities
- to deny the opposition scoring opportunities
- to have the fitness to sustain effort throughout the game
- to have the speed and skill to respond effectively within the context of the game.

Skill areas:
- attack – to be in appropriate position to shoot, pass or move with the ball
- defence – to be in an appropriate position to regain possession of the ball
- to move with the ball under control towards the target

- to pass the ball with accuracy to a team mate
- to shoot with accuracy and power at a target
- to challenge for the ball (i.e. tackling)
- to prevent the opposition from receiving the ball (i.e. marking)
- to prevent the ball from reaching a player or target (i.e. intercepting)
- to encourage involvement of all the children through the playing of small-sided games (e.g. three versus three or four versus four)
- to promote tactical awareness, sound decision making and good skill execution.

Over-the-net Category of Games

Intentions:
- to send the object into the opposing court so that it cannot be returned to land in your court
- to reach a predetermined score before your opponent(s).

Demands:
- to manoeuvre opponent(s) so as to create space
- to send the object so that it is difficult to return
- to cover your own court area, denying space to the opposition
- to have the agility to respond effectively to the needs of the game.

Skill areas:
- to place the object accurately behind, in front or to the side of your opponent
- to use accuracy, power, spin and disguise at appropriate times
- to return to a central position after playing the object
- to react quickly and decisively to the needs of the game.

Striking and Fielding Category of Games

Intentions:
- to strike an object
- to have a higher score than your opponents, at the end of the game
- to score by running to fixed markers or by some other method.

Demands:
- to strike the object
- to score before fielders can return the ball
- to 'get the batter out' or prevent him/her from scoring.

Skill areas:

- to strike the object away from the fielders
- to assess the various options and select an appropriate action
- to respond quickly and decisively to the quality of the strike
- to field effectively by tracking the object and returning it effectively to the main area of play.

In the primary school the focus of the games curriculum should be on helping children develop key skills to enable them to play adult versions of recognized games when they are older.

Key Skills and Key Words

Games skills are described using the key words **send**, **receive** and **travel with**. Figure 2.1 shows what these generic terms can encompass. (See also Study Sheet 1, Chapter 7.)

In early years teaching, it is important to remember that the children do not come to school without any experience of these skills (see Figure 2.2). They will have already experienced many of them through their natural development and through play. (See also Study Sheet 2, Chapter 7.)

Rolling   Aiming   Fielding

Striking   Dribbling   Gathering   Controlling

TRAVELLING

Spatial awareness

SENDING   **RECEIVING**

Agility

Footwork

Travelling

Kicking   Bouncing   Catching   Stopping

Pushing   Throwing   Trapping

FIGURE 2.1   Key skills and key words

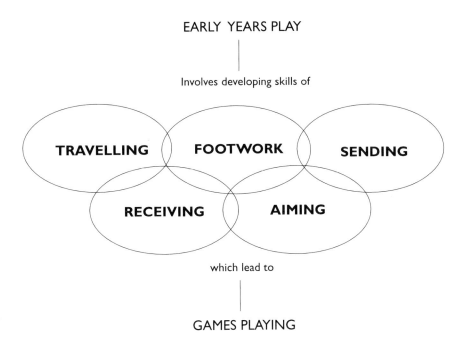

FIGURE 2.2   Early years play

Planning and Teaching for Games Skills Development

At the primary level, games teaching should focus on developing skills from all three categories of games and on using a wide variety of equipment. The skills require not only physical competence but also maturity, experience and cognitive development. For instance, many 5-year-old children can catch a large light-weight ball if it is thrown very carefully into their outstretched arms by a sympathetic adult, but there is no comparison between that and how in cricket a first-class wicket keeper might catch a ball.

All games skills, not just catching, need to be developed according to the current ability of each child. For many children, teachers begin too far along the journey of a skill and a practice on catching, for instance, can soon become a practice on dropping and retrieving. Children who continually meet failure in this way soon become unhappy, demoralized, unmotivated and often a discipline problem for their teachers.

Teachers need to be aware of the way in which what can seem to be simple skills (when you can do them!) actually develop.

Possible Journey of the Skill of Throwing

Holding
Releasing
Dropping
Bouncing
Rolling
Throwing with a number of bounces
Throwing with one bounce
Throwing without bounces
Various types of throw

> underarm
>
> overarm
>
> two handed, etc.

The list above suggests a developmental order on which the various aspects of throwing might be focused during planning and teaching the games curriculum in the early years. All the skills in the list above may be adapted to make them more or less challenging to meet the needs of children up to the end of Key Stage 2.

Suggestions for Adaptation and Differentiation within the Journey of a Skill

Any skill can be made more or less challenging (differentiated) by adding one or a number of these suggestions for adaptation.

Space: still or on the move   Most skills like rolling, catching or kicking are easier to do whilst staying in one place. Others, like hopping or bouncing a ball individually, are less challenging when some travelling is encouraged.

Distance: close together or far apart   There is often an optimum distance for each skill at different levels of development. For instance, in throwing and catching to and from a partner, too far apart may mean that the throw does not reach the partner or becomes wildly inaccurate, whilst too close together does not give the catcher sufficient time to make the necessary judgements about speed, direction, force and trajectory in order to catch successfully. Allowing children to decide their own spacing, under the teacher's guidance, can be useful.

Equipment: larger/smaller ball, lighter/heavier bat   A medium-sized ball of medium weight is less challenging to catch, strike or kick than a very small, light or very heavy ball. A heavy bat (e.g. a wooden one) is difficult for a young child to manage. The length of the handle is important too. Young children are still learning about exactly where their bodies start and end, which is why when given a long-handled racquet (like a traditional badminton or tennis racquet) they do not hold it by the hand grip but close to the head. Light-weight bats with shorter handles are useful in primary schools, particularly during the early years.

Direction: forwards, sideways, backwards   Catching a ball thrown from in front of you is far easier than catching one thrown from one side of you. Dribbling a ball with your feet in a straight line is much easier than having to twist and turn as you control the ball.

Level: light, medium, low   It is more challenging to receive a ball that has been sent towards you by a partner at knee height, or above your head, than one that has been sent at waist height.

Speed· quickly, slowly   Increase in speed usually means decrease in skill level. An example of this is how skills that have been practised individually with competence, break down when applied to situations where there is a time limit or competition from an opponent.

Force: hard, soft   As a fielder, it is more challenging to stop a ball that has been struck very hard than one that has been struck more gently.

Body parts used: feet, one hand, two hands   Some children (particularly girls in our culture) tend to move a ball or beanbag along with their hands and unless specifically required to do so, may not choose to use their feet. Children should be encouraged to use a variety of body parts.

With other people: partners, very small group, small group   Additional players mean that the number of possibilities are increased and so the decisions that have to be made also increase. For instance, in a game where two children are passing a ball to each other whilst another tries to touch the ball, (i.e. two versus one) the addition of another child (i.e. three versus one) increases the decisions that both the 'passers' and the 'touchers' must make.

Combination of skills: linking actions, stopping and starting   A child may be able to roll a ball accurately but when asked to receive a thrown ball and then roll it accurately in another direction, finds the combination of skills and decisions to be made much more challenging.

With opposition   A child may be skilful at dribbling and then kicking to a target or goal, but is greatly challenged by an opponent who is trying to gain possession of the ball and a goal keeper guarding the target.

In planning and teaching games (see Figure 2.3), sensitive use of these adaptations based on observation and assessment of the children's abilities will offer challenges to all children. Differentiation based on children's needs will encourage achievement, progression and positive attitudes towards games. (See Study Sheets 3 and 4, Chapter 7.)

Competition

The place of competition in school games teaching has led to much discussion and dissension. Teachers must remember that competition is an essential component of games, and pupils must be introduced to winning and losing. However, it is essential that teachers manage competition appropriately, drawing a balance between cooperation and competition, success and failure, ensuring that all children experience and can cope with all possible outcomes.

with different parts ____ keeping apparatus ____ sending apparatus ____ receiving from ____ receiving from
of the body   close to body   away   a partner   one of a group

to do one action ____ to do two actions ____ to do a number of actions

Use a
variety of ____ in own space _____ travelling in own space _____ travelling in
apparatus   forwards   forwards   general space
               sideways   sideways   forwards
               backwards   backwards   sideways
                                                                              backwards

to work slowly _____ more quickly _____ quickly _____ very quickly

individually _____ with a partner _____ cooperatively ____ competitively with a
                                               with a small group small group

FIGURE 2.3 Planning for a progressive games programme

NOTE: This figure highlights how differentiation and challenge can be implemented to encourage progression in skills development and develop understanding

Teachers need to remember that:

- individual potential is the uppermost priority in all teaching
- lessons should permit maximum time for active participation and skill development for all children
- the result of the game is of secondary importance – effective and appropriate use of skills, strategies and problem solving are the most important things
- all children should experience success
- whenever introduced, competition should be against yourself or between pairs or groups of equal ability, who have gained the basic skills beforehand
- a wide variety of competitive situations encourages personal awareness and appropriate responses

■ there is a logical progression from 'beat your own score' to one-versus-one cooperation and competition, through unequal sided games to four versus four, five versus five, etc.

■ use of progression encourages skill development and understanding, but rushing to a game similar to the adult form will usually handicap the majority of children.

Lesson Planning in Games

Every games lesson should include time for warm-up activities, skill development and a concluding cool-down activity. However, this does not mean that all games lessons will be structured in exactly the same way. Three different examples of possible structures for lesson planning in games are given below.

Possible Structure of a Games Lesson in the Early Years

Warm up   Make sure this is lively, warming, active and fun. It should also include some travel around the space available and should link with the activities later in the lesson.

Development of skills   Include footwork activities and activities using small apparatus. In the early years this section needs to include opportunities for children to explore the equipment as well as to be guided by their teachers. Towards the middle of Key Stage 1, this section will include some exploration but needs to focus on skill development, which could lead to simple paired games. In the last year of Key Stage 1, this section will include skills development, simple paired games and small-group work.

Concluding activity   Devise a whole-class activity with some discussion of the children's learning and experiences during the lesson. This should match the learning objectives in teachers' planning.

A Traditional Lesson Plan for Key Stage 2 Games

Warm up   Include free practice with a variety of equipment, vigorous warm-up, e.g. running, jumping, flexing, bending and revision of the previous games lesson.

Development of skills   Include individual skills that are essential for all games and can then be practised with a partner or in small groups, e.g. throwing and catching, striking – using various parts of the body and a variety of implements – and travelling with a variety of balls.

Application of a single skill   Having worked on developing a skill, and having practised it individually, with a partner and in a small group, the children are put in a games situation. Anything from one versus one, to two versus one, to three versus one, to three versus two, to a probable maximum of six versus six.

Concluding activity   Devise a whole-class activity with some discussion of the children's learning and experiences during the lesson. This should match the teachers' learning objectives.

An Alternative Lesson Plan for Key Stage 2 Games

Warm up   Tell the children what will be taught during the lesson and include a vigorous 'warm-up' activity to prepare the children for the physical nature of the lesson. This could be a revision of what they had learned in the previous lesson.

Small-sided games   Organize the children into groups ready to play small-sided games. Anything up to four versus four may be appropriate. Identify a few basic rules, e.g. how to play, how to score, how to restart, and then get the children playing. Move around the various groups acting as a resource or as a catalyst. Teachers may have to sort out problems or disputes but more importantly, they should make children think about what they are doing through a range of teaching styles.

Basic rules, equipment or the playing area for some groups may need to be adapted so that they are appropriate for all players.

Development of skills In this alternative plan, teaching skills is not being forgotten or ignored. Skills will be taught, but only when it is relevant and appropriate to the individual. Skills will most often be taught to some of the children while the rest of the class carry on playing. Class teaching will still have its place, but it should be used only sparingly.

Concluding activity Include some individual activities and some discussion of what the children have learned and experienced during the lesson.

No matter what lesson-planning structure is used, priority must be given to safety, differentiation, management and organizational strategies that offer maximum participation for all children and teaching points based on lesson objectives and teachers' observations.

Teaching Strategies

Whatever lesson structure is adopted by the teacher, a variety of teaching strategies should be adopted (see Figure 2.4). At Key Stage 1, it is likely that teachers will need to provide opportunities for familiarization with the equipment and experimentation by each child alongside some direct teaching. At Key Stage 2, teachers are more likely to use direct teaching to develop skills, together with a questioning approach to develop understanding of the principles of the game being played, e.g. 'Where would be a good place to stand to receive the ball?'

No single teaching strategy can be wholly effective and teachers need to suit their strategy to their learning objectives. Encouraging the development of creativity, understanding tactics and refining skills all need a different approach by the teacher.

Teaching Games

Teaching Points

Although the setting of appropriate, differentiated tasks will go some way

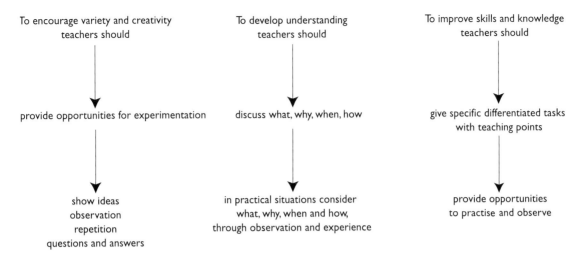

FIGURE 2.4   Range of teaching strategies for games

towards developing skills and ensuring progression, teachers must not only organize the children but must also actively **teach**. In games this most often means offering feedback via teaching points to individuals, small groups or the whole class, giving the children focused information in small doses, which will help them to be more effective at what they are doing, for example, 'When rolling a ball, swing your arm backwards to gain greater speed and force'.

Often, teaching points are most effective when supported by demonstrations by the teacher or other children, as visual representation makes more impact than verbal input alone.

At the individual lesson-planning stage, it is important to consider teaching and learning objectives, the series of activities being planned and then to formulate the teaching points that are likely to be needed. During the lesson, of course, teachers need to observe the children carefully and then decide which teaching points are appropriate to aid progress.

Inexperienced teachers can find it difficult to actually observe the children's movements in order to give feedback and teaching points, as in their early days they are often more concerned with managing behaviour and maintaining an ordered, safe environment. This is understandable but they should set themselves targets to give feedback and offer a few teaching points each lesson until this becomes a natural and developing part of their practice in teaching games or any other area of physical education.

The following notes on the basic skills of throwing and catching may help teachers become more aware of the range of aspects of the action that they might observe closely and then formulate appropriate teaching points.

Observing Throwing

Many games require the ability to throw for length and accuracy. This skill is normally performed using the arms and hands, with the body in a side-on stance and the body weight being transferred in the direction of the 'target'. A whole range of different throws exist and children find the skill challenging and enjoyable.

When the skill is being performed the following points should be observed:

- Where is the target?
- Is the child looking at the target?
- How high does the object travel?
- At what point does the child release the object?
- Where did the throwing action start?
- How many hands are being used? If one, which one?
- Are the child's feet properly positioned to help him/her to balance? (i.e. in an over-arm throw, the opposite leg should be forward to the throwing arm)
- Does the weight move in the direction of the throw?
- Does the child throw with a bent or a straight arm?
- Does the child follow through to the target with the throwing hand/hands?
- Does the child use the correct type of throw?

What you may see initially	*What you hope to see*
Little power or strength	Sufficient power in throw
Inappropriate point of release	Appropriate point of release
Little accuracy	Accurate throws to target
'Square on' body position	'Side on' body position
Short, quick arm action	Fluent arm action
Unbalanced finish	Balanced finish with feet ready to perform next action

Observing Catching

Many games use this skill and it should be taught to all children. However, it is a complex skill requiring complex cognitive judgements as well as sufficiently developed motor skills. It must be taught early in a child's physical education programme since many other games skills require the ability to catch before they can be developed.

Begin with beanbags or large soft balls and then progress to balls of different sizes. Generally, the smaller or harder the object, the more difficult it is to catch. Have a selection of balls of different sizes and weights available.

When the skill is being performed the following points must be observed:

■ Are the children watching the pathway (trajectory) of the object to be caught?
■ Where are the hands being held?
■ Are the hands and fingers pointing towards the object and ready to catch?
■ How many hands are being used to catch?
■ Are they able to judge the timing?
■ When catching, are the children snatching or reaching and giving?
■ Is the child well balanced when trying to catch?

What you may see initially	*What you hope to see*
Failure to catch ball cleanly	Good clean catching
Ball hitting hands and bouncing away	Hands and arms giving on catching
Child not watching approaching object	Child watching object to be caught
Hands, arms and upper body much too rigid	Moving to get into line or under the ball
Body off balance as catch is made	Feet well placed to balance body
Attempt to catch ball much too early, too close, too far away	Catch being made at appropriate time

(See Study Sheet 5, Chapter 7.)

Effective Management of Children, Equipment and the Games Environment

Children

In order to achieve a purposeful working atmosphere in games, as in all areas of physical education, it is important to remember that the lesson begins as the children collect their physical education kit, change and move to the playground, field or hall for their lesson. Teachers should set high expectations of children's behaviour during this phase of the lesson by establishing firm rules and routines. The tone of the whole lesson is set before it even begins.

It can be useful to explain the first activity before the children leave the classroom so that they can begin to work as soon as they reach the working space. It can also be useful to remind the children what they were focusing on in the previous lesson and give a brief outline of today's activities.

In order to make the most effective use of the time available, some schools have the children already organized into physical education groups. These may be similar to their classroom-based groups, friendship groups, ability groups or a mixture of all three. Physical education offers good opportunities for children to work closely with those children with whom they have little contact in the classroom environment. Some schools use colours to name their groups, which can be useful when assigning children to equipment (see the following section on equipment).

In general, children enjoy being active and are keen and cooperative during their physical education lessons. However, this can evaporate if they are expected to spend too long listening to instructions, waiting for their turn, or being organized by their teachers. Try to aim for the maximum time to be spent on physical activity for every child.

Equipment

The amount and range of games equipment that schools have varies enormously, but good management of the storage of that equipment is a great support to the busy teacher who does not have the time to untangle skipping ropes and put balls back into their storage crates before every lesson.

A colour-coded storage system is very simple and effective throughout the primary school. It is helpful in reinforcing concepts of colour and number in the early years, for establishing safe class routines and for ensuring that a range of equipment is available for each lesson. Four baskets/boxes (red, yellow, green and blue) might each contain large balls (both spherical and rugby-shaped), medium-sized balls, a variety of small balls (tennis, airflow, foam), wooden and plastic bats of different shapes, sizes and weights, skipping ropes (useful for marking out lines, nets or circles or targets), beanbags, quoits, markers and perhaps coloured bands for the children to wear. The ideal would be to have sufficient equipment for all the class to work individually.

For safety, each basket or box should be placed at a corner of the playing area. If children are already grouped into four colour groups then the organization of collecting and returning equipment during the lesson is simple, safe and fast, e.g. 'Yellow group, please put your balls back into your basket and collect a different piece of equipment that you could throw to your own target'.

Some schools store their equipment in baskets/boxes of similar equipment, i.e. all small wooden bats together, all cricket-type bats together, all short-handled racquets together. This can work well, but teachers need to ensure that children gain experience of using a variety of equipment and that the collecting and returning of equipment is carefully organized in a staggered way, so as to avoid a 'mad scramble' to one place by thirty children!

A word of caution – remember to check that the equipment required for your lesson is available and in working order. Planning a lesson including the use of large balls and then finding out that they are all flat, is not fun. Also, at the end of your lesson make sure that all the equipment is returned to the baskets/boxes and that these are put away tidily. Leaving the games cupboard or shed in a complete mess will not endear you to other staff.

Environment

The school playground or field is the most appropriate space for teaching primary games. The school hall could be used if the weather is particularly bad but the lack of space will hamper children's development and make the teacher's task more difficult, with adaptations probably being necessary to the planned outdoor lesson.

Some early years teachers feel that the children might get too cold outside, but if their lessons are active, then this should not be a problem. Schools should consider what is appropriate clothing for primary games. Sweatshirts and track-suit bottoms or leggings should be available for wearing outdoors.

With all age groups it is important to limit the outdoor teaching area either by using existing features, such as the hedge/trees/games shed or by the use of markers or ropes. Figure 2.5 shows a netball court divided lengthways. It gives a suitable space with six small teaching areas.

For safety

- Remember to place boxes/baskets of equipment outside or on the perimeter of the teaching space.
- Check the surface of the teaching space. Wet leaves or a gritty surface can be dangerous.
- If the lesson involves striking activities, ensure that the direction of the strikes is away from the general teaching space.

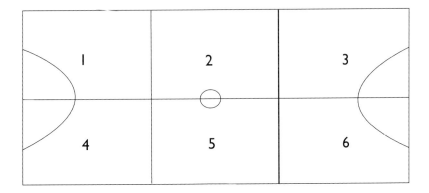

FIGURE 2.5   A netball court divided lengthways provides six small teaching areas

Effective Games Teaching at Key Stage 1

Effective games teaching at Key Stage 1 requires teachers to:

- encourage active exploration and experimentation using a variety of equipment alone, in pairs and very small groups
- sometimes let the children choose the equipment they will use in exploratory tasks
- encourage free use of all the space within a designated area
- assist children to be aware of other children when moving in a designated area and when sending balls away or swinging a bat/stick
- introduce direct teaching alongside exploratory work to help children develop their skills
- encourage children to link their actions together, e.g. roll, chase and pick up a ball. This will later develop to moving objects and/or persons
- help children to measure their progress through participation in a variety of skill challenges, e.g. how many, how far, how quickly, how accurately?
- introduce simple paired games activities as soon as pupils are able to cooperate/compete with a partner, e.g. throw underarm to a wall for partner to catch after one bounce.

What Teachers Should Know to Teach Games at Key Stage 1

In order to teach games at Key Stage 1, teachers should:

- have a repertoire of basic actions and skills for sending, receiving and travelling
- know what children need to do to perform those skills proficiently and safely
- know how to observe children's actions in order to give appropriate teaching points to aid progression
- have a repertoire of many practice tasks and skill challenges in which children have fun and can experience success
- be able to devise and organize simple games
- be able to simplify and extend (differentiate) games activities to offer appropriate levels of challenge for different abilities
- be able to manage large groups in an open space so that children may work freely, actively and safely
- know how to manage equipment safely and effectively.

What Teachers Should Know to Teach Games Effectively at Key Stage 2

To teach games effectively at Key Stage 2 teachers are required to:

- use a number of small-sided and simplified versions of games rather than one large game to increase active involvement for all and to promote healthy competition;
- adopt class-management strategies, which include many smaller games, i.e. avoid playing one game of rounders with the teacher bowling!;
- position four/five small-side games in a 'circular' or a North, South, East, West formation from a central area or in each area of a divided netball court
- ensure that children understand or develop the structure, rules and safety procedures for each game so they can assume some responsibility for running their own games;
- assist children to understand how rules shape a game and determine what they may or may not do. For example, get children to play a throw–catch game in which players may only take two steps with the ball in their hands, then play the game so that they can bounce or dribble the ball, and explore how these change the tactics within the game;
- help children understand the principles of games playing, e.g. of attack and defence. They need to understand game objectives and what they are expected to do to achieve those objectives. When pressed for time, it is easy for teachers to say 'Just stand over there' and then wonder why a pupil does not react to the play;
- aim to help each child to work to their own skill threshold by differentiating tasks, e.g. instead of all dribbling a ball out to a line, ask children to judge how far they think they can dribble in 5–6 seconds, yet still dribble back before the time is up. Help them by calling out the seconds.

What Teachers Should Know to Teach Games at Key Stage 2

In order to teach games at Key Stage 2, teachers should be able to:

- understand the common objectives of games within each category, i.e. invasion, over the net, fielding and striking
- observe children's actions in order to give appropriate teaching points to aid progression
- impose and change rules to shape different types of game for different purposes
- design practice tasks in order to work towards achieving teaching and learning objectives

- help children develop understanding, responsibility and sensitivity as they play competitive games
- devise many practice tasks and skill challenges in which children can have fun and achieve success
- simplify and extend (differentiate) games activities to offer appropriate challenges to children with different abilities
- manage large groups in an open space so that all are safe, challenged and yet achieve success
- manage equipment safely and effectively.

'TOPS' Programmes

The Top Play and BT Top Sport Games initiatives will have been introduced to the majority of primary schools in the country by 2002. These provide training for teachers, equipment and resource cards.

The Top Play Programme

The TOP Play Programme is designed for use with primary-age children with emphasis on 4–9-year-olds. The programme uses resource cards to bring a variety of games activities to children. The cards have been developed by the Youth Sport Trust and the Sports Council and have been carefully designed so they:

- can be used by children
- support the National Curriculum
- offer a variety of linked activities
- include activities that can be set up quickly and easily
- give useful hints to teachers on:
    safety
    how the cards apply to the National Curriculum;
    organizing the activities
    equipment
    follow-up games.

TOP Play cards are not sport specific but concentrate on the core games skills that younger children need. The cards are currently available in the following categories:

Rolling
Receiving
Travelling with a ball

Running and jumping
Throwing and catching
Striking
Kicking.

The cards within each category are progressive, using simple activities first and then moving on to simple games involving a small number of children. The cards are supported by bags of equipment, carefully designed for children and providing the necessary resources to play the games safely.

All schools involved in TOP Play need to use the official cards and equipment. A scheme trainer will have ensured that teachers from the school receive training on the use of the cards. The training is designed to allow people to experience the games and to think about how to integrate them with the school's curriculum planning.

The BT TOP Sport Programme

The BT TOP Sport Programme is designed for use with primary-age children with emphasis on 7–11-year-olds.

The programme uses resource cards to bring a variety of linked games activities to children. The cards have been developed by the Youth Sport Trust and Loughborough University with help from the Sports Council, the National Governing Bodies of Sport, the PEA (UK) and BAALPE (British Association of Advisors and Lecturers in Physical Education). They have been carefully designed so that they:

- can be used by children
- support the National Curriculum
- offer a variety of linked activities
- include games that can be set up quickly and easily
- give useful hints to teachers on:
     safety
     adapting the games
     how the cards apply to the National Curriculum
     equipment
     follow-up games.

BT TOP Sport cards are sport specific. The cards are currently available in the following sports:

Basketball
Cricket
Hockey

Netball
Rugby
Table Tennis
Tennis.

The cards are linked, using simple activities first and then moving on to more complex games and are supported by equipment packages, carefully designed for children and providing the necessary equipment to carry out the games safely. All schools involved in BT TOP Sport need to use the official cards and equipment. A scheme trainer will have ensured that teachers from the school receive training on the use of the cards. The training is designed to allow people to experience the games and to think about how to integrate them with the school's curriculum planning.

In many areas TOP Play and BT TOP Sport are well established and a wide range of other TOPS programmes, which focus on other areas of physical education for ages 18 months to 11 years, are being developed. Your local education authority, physical education advisor or sports development officer should be able to give you details of arrangements for TOPS training and initiatives in your local area.

GYMNASTIC ACTIVITIES

Gymnastics in the primary school is concerned with children developing the basic actions of travelling on hands and feet, jumping, rolling, balancing, climbing and using the floor and where possible, apparatus (see Study Sheet 6, Chapter 7). These actions should be linked to form sequences in which the end of one movement becomes the beginning of the next movement.

The QCA document *Maintaining Breadth and Balance* states that in gymnastic activities, by the end of Key Stage 1 most children should be able to:

■ perform the basic actions of travelling, rolling, jumping, balancing, climbing and swinging using the floor and apparatus;
■ link actions together both on the floor and using apparatus.

By the end of Key Stage 2, most children should be able to:

■ perform different ways of jumping, rolling, turning and balancing, travelling on hands and feet, and climbing and swinging, emphasizing changes of shape, speed and direction;
■ plan and perform more complex sequences both on the floor and apparatus.

It is not only important that children are able to do these basic actions, but also that the quality of their movements is developed. By using a variety of body parts and body shapes, appropriate body tension and changes of speed, direction and levels, children should be able to develop quality of movement in the basic actions and also develop more creativity, control and a wider movement vocabulary. Clearly children's physical development is an important factor for teachers to consider and through gymnastics, children should maintain and develop their strength, endurance, flexibility, balance and spatial awareness.

Exploring the Basic Gymnastic Actions

Travelling

Travelling in gymnastics means moving from one place to another. This can be done in innumerable ways but the most common, particularly in the early years, is by using feet or hands and feet. However, even when using only feet or hands and feet there are many possible variations. Here are just a few involving travelling on the feet and hands:

stepping	galloping
walking	striding
running	jumping
hopping	leaping
skipping	playing hopscotch

The following involve travelling on hands and feet:

stepping	bunny jumping
walking	performing a low cartwheel
running	performing a full cartwheel

Stepping, walking and running can all be done on one foot and two hands or one hand and two feet or two hands and two feet with the back facing the ceiling or when lying on the floor.

Jumping

Although jumping is a basic action, it cannot be considered in isolation. Landing is just as important! It is important to teach both landing and preparation for jumping. To teach landing before jumping itself enables children to know how to complete the action safely and resiliently. Landing on two feet should be taught first. When landing from apparatus, all landings should be symmetrical onto both feet, flexing the ankles, knees and hips and then springing back up to a standing position (see Study Sheet 7, Chapter 7).

Within the basic action of jumping there are many variations. The children will definitely create more, given the opportunity:

from two feet to two feet
from right foot to two feet
from left foot to two feet
from two feet to left foot
from two feet to right foot
from right foot to right foot (hop)
from left foot to left foot (hop)
from right foot to left foot (leap)
from left foot to right foot (leap).

When teaching jumping, focus your observation and teaching points on the preparation, the take-off, the position and body shape in the air and the landing.

Rolling

Rolling is the ability to transfer the body weight smoothly from one body surface to the next adjacent body surface, along the floor or apparatus, often turning through 360°.

Most rolls can be performed on the floor or on, off or along apparatus. Some rolls, such as the forward and backward rolls, are more comfortably practised and refined on mats or shallow ramps until the gymnast has achieved competence and resilience.

There are many types of roll and children will always create more, but the most common are:

■ lying in a stretched (extended) shape and then rolling sideways to right and left (sometimes referred to as a log, pin, pencil or sausage roll)
■ kneeling in a curled (flexed) shape and then rolling sideways to right and left (tucked or egg roll)
■ sitting in straddle (wide extended legs), holding the legs and then rolling sideways to right and left (circle roll)
■ lying in a curved, extended shape and then rolling forwards and backwards (dish or hollow roll)

- kneeling on one knee with the other leg extended to the side and then rolling sideways to right or left, to finish on the other knee
- standing in straddle, placing the hands flat on mat a shoulder width apart, bending elbows with control, tucking the head through the legs and placing the shoulders on mat thus rolling forwards onto the seat or onto the feet (straddle forward roll)
- standing, then bending the legs (squatting) and then rolling forwards onto the seat or feet (forward roll)
- squatting, then rolling backwards over one shoulder to the kneeling position (backwards roll)
- squatting, then rolling backwards to a straddle stand (backwards roll to straddle)
- squatting, then rolling backwards to a squatting position (backwards roll to a tucked position).

In forward rolls common difficulties and mistakes can be overcome by telling the children to place their hands flat, with their palms down on the mat, keep their knees wide apart and tuck their heads between their legs (see Study Sheet 7).

Balancing

This action involves holding the body weight in a still position over the base. To help children to develop a rich vocabulary of ways of balancing, it can be useful to teach them to categorize each type of balance according to its base. The most common bases are:

large bases	front, back, side, shoulders
small bases	feet, hip, knees, elbows, hands
using many body parts as a base	two hands and two feet, or seat plus feet and hands, or one knee and one foot
using few body parts as a base	seat and one foot, or one hand and one foot, or one knee and one foot
body near to the base	lying on the back in a tucked shape, or in a tucked shape and kneeling
body far from the base	shoulder balance, or standing on one foot with the other leg, body and arms outstretched, or performing a headstand
body directly over the base	standing, or performing a headstand
body leaning away from the base	standing on two feet and one hand or two hands and one foot
the right way up	sitting tucked or kneeling

upside down

performing a headstand, or with two feet and two hands with either the front or the back facing towards the ceiling.

For each of the above pairs of categories, it is usually easier to learn the first category before the second. For example, large bases are usually more stable and less challenging than small bases. All these categories can be very useful in providing a variety of activities. A class of children when asked to explore balancing techniques will probably use some of those suggested above and the teacher can then suggest other categories in order to widen their movement vocabulary and offer further challenges.

Turning

This action involves the whole body changing direction. Turning involves rotating through an axis. The three most common axes of rotation are longitudinal, dorsi-central and horizontal.

Longitudinal axis Imagine a pin going from head to foot through the body. Using this axis children can roll over sideways, lying down or can jump to turn, or can spin to turn on one foot, or on their seat.

Dorsi-central axis   Imagine a pin going through the centre of the body from front to back. Using this axis children can spin whilst lying on their fronts or backs, or can perform cartwheels.

Horizontal axis   Imagine a pin going in from the left side of the body, through the centre and out at the right side. Using this axis children can rock on their backs, roll forwards or backwards or on apparatus, or they can circle around a horizontal pole.

Twisting

Twists can easily be confused with turns but analysis will show that they are different movements. A twist is an action in which part of the body is fixed and the rest of the body changes direction. Examples of twisting would be:

■ from a kneeling position, twisting at the waist to move to a sitting position
■ from a shoulder balance, twisting at the waist and placing the knees over one shoulder to land on the knees
■ from a standing position, bunny jumping and twisting to land on the feet, with the feet in a new place.

Swinging

This action can only be practised on apparatus such as a horizontal pole, or a rope. It is important that children can grip securely with their hands and take their own weight whilst hanging from their hands before teaching them to swing on a rope. Check, too, that they have sufficient space to ensure safety and that they know how to land.

Climbing

This is another action requiring apparatus such as a climbing frame, a ladder, a movement table, a rope or an inclined bench. Children should learn to climb up and down from apparatus and where appropriate, to climb across, along, over, through and under apparatus.

   All the basic actions described above should be taught and developed so that children accumulate a wide movement vocabulary and learn to perform individual movements and sequences that show:

■ increasing body and spatial awareness
■ increasing quality in body tension and efficiency of movement
■ a range of body shapes and body parts being used

- greater use of variation in speed, direction and level
- appropriate posture and use of the body
- an awareness of their own safety and that of others
- resilience in landing (encourage children to listen to their landings in order to develop 'soft' quiet landings).

Developing Basic Gymnastic Actions

In order to extend their movement vocabulary, it is not enough for children only to be taught and to experience the basic gymnastic actions. It is also important that they are taught and experience a variety of ways in which the basic actions can be developed and adapted. The body parts being used, body shape, levels, direction, speed, pathways and relationships with other gymnasts can all be used to adapt and develop the basic actions (see Figure 2.6).

Body shape   This might be stretched (extended), tucked (flexed), twisted, wide, long, symmetrical, or asymmetrical.

Body parts   Some children need encouragement to consider using body parts other than their hands and feet. Teachers need to encourage them to use their hips, legs, knees, arms, shoulders, back, front, right side and left side.

Levels   Using a mixture of low, medium and high movements adds variety and challenge to individual actions and sequences.

Pathways   Straight, curved and zigzag pathways which travel towards, away from and around other gymnasts or apparatus add a further dimension to children's movement vocabulary.

Direction   Forwards, backwards, sideways right, sideways left, up and down movements within an action or sequence adds interest and challenge.

Speed   A variety of speed, acceleration, deceleration and stillness requires gymnasts to use increasing levels of body control and body tension and should be encouraged at all stages of development.

Relationships   Whilst in the early years, children will usually work individually, opportunities for working with a partner or in small groups will offer new learning experiences both related to gymnastic skills and personal communication and social skills.

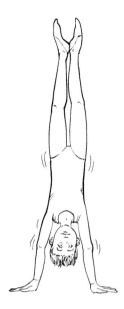

Linking Actions into Sequences

Linking gymnastic actions and building sequences are important elements in helping children to develop a wide movement vocabulary and movement memory and to become skilful and creative gymnasts. Children should be encouraged to link actions together from an early age. A relatively simple sequence of 'jump, land, jump, land' can be achieved by 5-year-olds.

It can be useful to help children retain quality in the second action by teaching them to use the ending of the first action as preparation for the second. For example, using the landing from the first jump as the preparation for the second maintains momentum and results in a smoother sequence. Some actions will require another action as a link between them. For example, adding a roll between jumping, landing (rolling) and balancing.

Encourage a wide vocabulary of ways of beginning each action. There are for example, numerous ways of moving into balancing on the shoulders. The basic action is:

■ from lying on the back, raising the legs vertically and then placing the hands on the hips to support the back.

The following list shows examples of different starting points that can then be followed by the basic action outlined above:

■ sitting and then rocking back

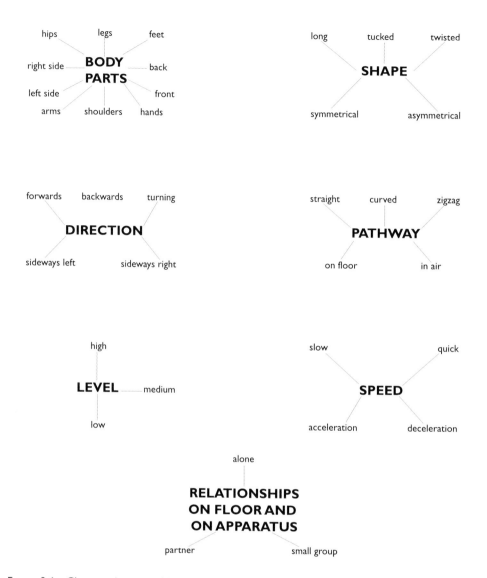

FIGURE 2.6   Chart to show possible development of basic gymnastic actions

- lying on the front, then rolling over onto the back
- standing, then bending the knees to sit and rock back
- standing on the hands and feet with the back facing the ceiling, lowering the body to lying on the front and rolling over onto the back
- standing on the hands and feet with the back facing the floor, turning onto the side, sliding the feet away to lie on the side and rolling over onto the back
- kneeling, twisting at the waist to lower the seat to the floor in a sideways sit, reaching with the hands to lower the body onto the side and rolling onto the back.

Encourage a wide vocabulary of ways of moving out of each basic action. There are for example, numerous ways of moving out of a forward roll:

- opening out to finish lying on the back and then rolling over to the front and finishing the roll in a sitting position
- tucking up to balance on the seat, twisting and flexing (bending) the knees to land in a quarter turn on the knees
- finishing the roll by flexing the knees, placing the feet near the seat, reaching forward with hands to help transfer weight and then standing
- opening the legs wide and extending (straightening) the knees to complete the roll sitting in the straddle position
- widening the legs as above, placing the hands in front of the seat and pushing up to stand in the straddle position
- finishing the first roll on the feet and continuing directly into a second forward roll or other action.

Encourage the children to use a wide variety of linking movements such as twists, which can also provide a change of direction in a sequence, for example:

- from a kneeling position, twisting to place the seat on the floor to continue into the next action
- from a squatting position, placing the hands flat on the floor and jumping, twisting at the waist to land with the feet in a new place (bunny jump with a twist)
- from a shoulder balance, bending the knees and twisting to place the knees over the shoulder onto the mat, whilst pushing with the hands on the mat beside the head.

Teach links that introduce contrasts of direction, speed, level, body shape and pathways. Some links add complexity to sequences by challenging the performance of the basic actions. Changes to the common beginnings and ends of basic actions lead to a greater variety of linking possibilities. For example:

- entering a forward roll from a one-foot balance and exiting by making a quarter turn to end in a kneeling position
- from a shoulder balance, placing the feet over the shoulders and pushing with the hands to slide the feet away to end in a front lying position
- running quickly to make a controlled entry into a leap
- from a headstand, pushing up to bunny jump or to a handstand.

When teaching children to link their movements into sequences, teachers will need to help them plan and evaluate their own performance, select links that extend their movement vocabulary and movement memory and challenge their skills, knowledge and understanding to produce sequences of ever increasing complexity and quality.

Working with Partners and in Small Groups

Before embarking on partner work or group work, teachers should ensure that children have a wide personal movement vocabulary of gymnastic actions, a well-developed memory of various movements and that they are able to plan, perform and evaluate their own work and evaluate the work of others.

Partners should be chosen carefully by the children and/or the teacher. It is also important that both partners continue to be physically active and not too much time is spent solely in discussion or observation. Partner work should be mainly non-contact but some able children might work towards contact partner work with a compatible partner.

Non-contact partner work might include:

- observing a partner and giving feedback
- leading and following, with partners taking turns in each role
- moving together or in canon
- working side by side, facing each other, back to back or a mixture of these
- working in a variety of directions such as towards each other, away from each other and around each other
- working over and under each other (but only body positions are stable), performing the same action or showing contrasting ways of performing.

Contact partner work might include:

- counter-balancing
- supporting some of the partner's weight
- supporting all of the partner's weight.

Partner work can be developed into small-group work with upper Key Stage 2 children. This makes increased demands on their spatial awareness, movement memory and personal communication skills.

Developing Quality in Gymnastics

By focusing on the following aspects of gymnastics, teachers will be able to help children to improve the quality of their work.

- body awareness – knowledge of and ability to use the limbs and the whole body effectively and with coordination;
- body fitness – use of appropriate strength, stamina, flexibility, tension;

- spatial awareness of both personal space (the space needed around the body at any time to produce the best-possible gymnastics) and general space (the entire space available in the hall) at low, medium and high levels, during warm-up, floor work and during apparatus work when the apparatus presents obstacles in that space;
- linking actions into sequences;
- resilience, fluency, control and efficiency in movement;
- developing their gymnastics vocabulary and memory of movements;
- developing their observation skills and the ability to interpret observations and adapt them for their own learning and development;
- giving appropriate, differentiated feedback;
- encouraging children to evaluate their own work and give feedback to others working individually and with a partner or in a small group;
- encouraging the use of the learning cycle of planning, performing and evaluating.

The following is an excerpt from 'Gymnastics in the Infant Curriculum', Cambridgeshire County Council (now out of print):

Quality improves when there is understanding of movement and appreciation of a good performance. It can be achieved by:

- expecting quality work and not accepting 'second best'
- encouragement and positive praise
- effective teaching points to make children aware of body shape and appropriate body action
- selecting good demonstrations
- training children in observation of quality during demonstration (the children then return to their activities with something positive to try)
- allowing time to repeat and practise known work
- extending the movement
- working for greater control
- maintaining the interest with variety in the work, e.g. introducing new apparatus arrangements.

Progression is made by:

- assessing the children's ability and experience and enabling the gymnast to assess his/her own ability, achievement and potential
- selecting and planning the teaching material carefully
- having high expectations of the children
- making intellectual and physical demands on the children
- working for quality and variety
- observation by teacher and children
- selecting work carefully for demonstration as it becomes appropriate
- evaluating fully – both by teacher and children.

Progression is also made by:

- making the skill more difficult, for example: higher/further, 'show a stretched shape in the jump'
- children making decisions within the variety of choice, for example: 'travel from one end of the bench to the other'
- the teacher narrowing the choice, for example: 'travel from one end of the bench to the other using hands and feet'
- combining activities to make a movement sequence, for example: 'run, jump, land and roll sideways'; 'come off your apparatus then take your weight onto your hands'
- progressing steadily from lesson to lesson to consolidate learning and develop confidence.

Without Progression Children Under-Achieve

Progression for Specific Gymnastic Skills

For many children, specific gymnastic actions are not easy to perfect. For example, the specific skills of forward rolls and handstands can present difficulties but can be made more achievable by learning skills which build towards them. This is rather like teaching children to read and spell simple consonant, vowel, consonant words like 'cat' before expecting them to manage complex words like 'catalogue'.

The actions listed in Table 2.1 will help children develop the skills needed to manage forward rolls and handstands. (See Study Sheet 8.)

Lesson Planning in Gymnastics

Each lesson should be part of a planned unit of work, covering perhaps half a term. The lessons should have clear teaching and learning objectives and a specific assessment focus linked to the objectives. Every gymnastics lesson should include time for warm-up activities, development of skills, preferably on the floor and apparatus, some sequencing work and a concluding, cool-down activity. A plan of the apparatus layout is also required.

It can be very helpful to start gymnastics sessions in the classroom by giving children the first task so that on entering the hall they can immediately start work on a 'warming-up' activity.

The warm-up phase need only take a few minutes, provided that the children are properly prepared. The warm-up should be spent in preparing the children's hearts and lungs, joints and muscles, concentration and motivation, spatial and body awareness, in readiness for the session to follow. It can be

TABLE 2.1 Suggested progressive activities that build towards achieving forward rolls and handstands

Forward roll	Handstand
extended sideways roll	Balances to learn stability
tucked sideways roll	on two hands and two feet
rolling from sitting	on two hands and one foot
rolling down a ramp	front support
rolling from apparatus to mat	side support right and left
rocking on the back	back support
rocking to stand up	
standing in a wide but stable straddle,	Shape – to learn extended, straight
place hands flat on floor in front,	shape of handstand
shoulder width apart, push body	
weight from feet to hands, flex elbows,	front lying
place shoulders on the mat, rock down	side lying right and left
the back to stand	back lying
from standing in squat, place hands	standing
as above	standing on balls of feet (with arms extended, shoulder-width apart, by ears)
	Inversion
	shoulder balance
	headstand
	bunny jump

useful to introduce the gymnastic activities that you intend to develop in the floor work during the warm-up phase.

Floor work should take about 10 or 15 minutes of a 40-minute session. It is useful to revise activities from previous sessions and introduce new challenges, often culminating in a sequence. Children need time to plan, perform and evaluate their work and to select, repeat and refine their gymnastic skills and sequences. The teacher's role is to observe the children and to provide feedback to help them to progress and achieve quality movements. Where appropriate, teachers should include demonstrations of children's work provided that the children observing are given a focus for their observations and this is followed briefly by discussion.

Apparatus work should take half the session and should enable the children to develop the gymnastic actions that they have developed during their floor work. These should be transferred, as appropriate, to the apparatus and should culminate in quality sequences.

Apparatus should be readily accessible around the hall, and should be lifted or wheeled and placed appropriately, by the children. The QCA document *Maintaining Breadth and Balance* (QCA, 1998) states that all children should be taught from Key Stage 1 to 'lift, carry and place equipment safely'.

Although the children should be given the opportunity to lift, carry and place their own apparatus from an early age, this will need careful management and they will need to be taught how to manage this. Teachers should always check that the apparatus has been safely set up before it is used and should encourage the children to take responsibility in this too.

Mats should be regarded as extensions of the apparatus and often suggest appropriate areas for dismounting from apparatus. Try to arrange the apparatus so that there are many points from which the children can start work. This avoids the need for children to queue and helps them to learn to travel towards, onto, off and away from apparatus and mats from a variety of starting and finishing points and with awareness for others.

It is advisable for children to take out and put away the same apparatus for several weeks, allowing them to become familiar with that apparatus set and consequently as they become more efficient, less time is spent managing the movement of apparatus.

For some teaching teachers may ask children to stay on a particular set of apparatus. On other occasions teachers may expect the children to move freely from one set of apparatus to another to fulfil the task. They should learn to manage both situations. Towards the end of Key Stage 2, children should be able to design and plan layouts for their own apparatus sets. This can provide useful links with design, technology and geography.

During apparatus work teachers should set tasks and give feedback in similar ways to the floor work and should encourage the children to plan, perform and evaluate their actions and sequences.

Concluding activities should follow the putting away of the apparatus and should serve as revision time, as time for reviewing what has been learnt, as time to consider posture and as time to relax and prepare for returning to the classroom. In the classroom teachers may ask the children to record their gymnastics or to design apparatus arrangements for future work.

Safety during Gymnastic Lessons

The best way to maximize safety in gymnastics is for teachers to have well-planned lessons that show careful consideration of organization and management.

Teachers need to consider a wide variety of aspects which may affect safety.

The environment:

■ changing area
■ hall:

floor – condition, surface
wall projections, e.g. pianos, chairs
lighting and ventilation
size in relation to the number of children and the activity.

The children:

■ stage of movement development
■ spatial awareness
■ previous experience
■ health, medical conditions and fitness
■ clothing and footwear
■ hair and accessories.

Procedure:

■ lesson structure
■ appropriate differentiated activities
■ relevant feedback/teaching points
■ suitable progressions
■ apparatus check: hooks, clamps, screws, proximity of sets to each other, walls, windows, etc.
■ lesson timing
■ class size
■ use of demonstration.

Apparatus:

■ lifting: suitable techniques and experience of children
■ carrying, placing and spacing
■ condition
■ choose apparatus to suit the age and size of the children and the content of the lesson.

Mats:

■ non-slip, flat and in sound condition
■ there should be no gaps between adjacent mats
■ mats should be placed to indicate area for dismounting.

TABLE 2.2   An example of a unit of work

Year 4, Key Stage 2, Time (no of lessons): 6 x 40 minutes

Title of unit: To plan, practise, improve and refine performance and evaluate travel and balance on floor and apparatus

Lesson structure	Lesson 1	Lesson 2	Lesson 3
Learning objectives	Physical activity Audit vocabulary of travel and balance actions	Develop control in balances, resilience in travel	Improve and evaluate balance on hands and travel on hands and feet
Assessment focus	Children to record own vocabulary of travel and balance actions in writing and/or pictures	Clarity and control in balances, resilience in travel	Ability to travel and balance on hands and feet and to evaluate these
Introduction	Practise different ways of travelling around the room using feet only: focus on three actions and check posture	Travel around the room in different directions on feet, then hands and feet	Travel from feet to hands to feet and back
Development – floorwork	Practise balances Sequence travel and balance	Balance on large, then small body parts Sequence of travel on hands and feet Balance on large body part, travel, balance on small body part Balance on many, then few body parts as base	Balance near to, then far from base Teach weight on hands to develop bunny jump and cartwheel
Development – apparatus work	Travel towards, onto, over, under, around and off the apparatus Sequence travel and balance	Use apparatus to assist balance on hands Sequence travel on hands and feet with balances	Use apparatus to assist balance on hands Sequence travel on hands and feet with balances
Conclusion	Review audit of travel, balance and posture	Practise new balances	Evaluate balance on hands

Resources: Hall with climbing frame, poles, ladder, trestles, stool, box, benches, movement tables, mats

Lesson 4	Lesson 5	Lesson 6
Improve and evaluate inverted balances	Evaluate a partner's posture, physical activity, travel and balance	Sequence balance and travel with a partner
Ability to balance upside down and to evaluate progress	Evaluation of a partner's best balances, travel, physical activity and posture	Children to record own achievements in balance and travel in writing and/or pictures
Travel over the floor from feet to hands to feet, concentrating on control of speeds and posture	Travel over the floor from feet to hands to feet, concentrating on linking movements together smoothly Check partner's physical activity and posture	Practise and refine short sequences of travel and balance
Upside-down balances Practise travel on feet and on hands and feet, developing bunny jump and cartwheel, sequencing with inverted balances	Practise and improve upside-down balances linked with travel, working alone. Make a sequence of new learning from this unit on travel and balance Refine and evaluate own sequence Perform sequence to a partner and evaluate together	Show sequence to partner. Select two travels and two balances Practise them as a non-contact partner sequence Perform sequence to another pair Evaluate each other
Use apparatus to assist upside-down balances. Link into sequences with rolling taught in previous units Sequence of two balances	Work alone to prepare a sequence of new learning from this unit of travel and balance Perform the sequence	Practise non-contact partner travel to apparatus, way of getting on, balance, dismount and travel away Perform sequence to another pair
Discuss and show partner 'best' balances and rolls		Evaluate the learning objectives of the unit

Learning Support Assistant (LSA) to work with child X

TABLE 2.3   An example of a lesson plan for Key Stage 1

Area of activity: Gymnastics;   *Unit of work*: Travelling on hands and feet;

Teaching and learning objectives: For children to develop their movement vocabulary, specifically improving techniques for travel on hands and feet, using the floor and apparatus with quality and control?

Date:	*Class*:	*Yr.* 1	*Age*: 5/6	*No. of children*: 30	*Duration*: 30 mins

Lesson structure and timing	*Progressive activities*	*Differentiation possibilities*
Warm-up, 2/3 mins	Bouncing, hopping, jogging, skipping on the spot On hands and feet to a new place, then bounce/hop/skip and then go somewhere else	Height off floor Tension in posture Speed of travel Resilience
Development floorwork, up to 15 mins	Roll across the floor Bunny jump on the spot and travel to new space on hands and feet Choose two ways of travelling, join them to make a sequence	Complexity of roll Speed of roll Height of bunny jump Variation in travel Link of sequence
Development apparatus, up to 20 mins	Getting out the apparatus. Safety check Get onto and off apparatus Travel to apparatus, get on, get off and travel away Choose one apparatus set. Travel to it, onto, off it and away from it. Put apparatus away	Ability to cooperate Variation in body parts and actions used
Cool-down, 2/3 mins	Revise travel sequence on floor Discuss travel techniques practised	

Lesson number: 3

Assessment focus: Can the children name two ways of travelling on hands and feet and demonstrate them?

Venue: Hall   *Resources*: Apparatus plan showing arrangement of fixed, portable apparatus and mats

---

Teaching points and feedback	Management and safety
Upright posture. Flex/extend encourages quiet feet on the floor Light feet as you go, eyes looking for spaces Springy hops, bounces, flat hands on floor	Check personal space for each child, use whole hall Keep clear of apparatus, doorways, walls Look for clear route and new space, avoid collisions
Extended/tucked smoothly, softly to right and left, change shape of leg pattern Hands flat, shoulder width apart, eyes looking forward, hands under shoulders Travel, back up, back down, turning over low cartwheel Encourage contrast of body parts used, smooth change-over, short distance for each	Roll away from others, change shape, direction to avoid collisions Feet kept low to help control landings Encourage children to plan, experiment, select, refine and practise their chosen sequence
Teach lifting, carrying, setting up, cooperation and control Use feet, hands and feet, set, front, knees as appropriate Try hands and feet to travel or bounce, hop, jog, gallop, skip on feet Start away from apparatus, light resilient travel to, smooth mount and dismount and travel away Remind children of lifting techniques, cooperation and safety	Allocate apparatus, children watching, listening Safe handling, spacing, placing and setting up Check all apparatus for safety (teacher and children) Everyone working – using all areas of apparatus Encourage care with spacing, avoid crowding – learn to look for available apparatus Encourage appropriate and safe selection of methods of travel, mounts and dismounts Clear instructions – safe handling Sit on floor when finished
Work softly, smoothly, looking for spaces for your two ways of travelling	Help children to remember content of sequence, link and spacing

The teacher:

■ should always be in a position to see the majority of the class
■ should use strong, clear starting and stopping signals
■ should be continually observing
■ should at least get the children to change into appropriate footwear or bare feet and should consider own clothing and accessories
■ should have a lesson plan that shows organizational considerations
■ should maintain close control
■ should be in constant attendance.

The most important factor in establishing and maintaining safety is to plan thoroughly, organize, manage and teach the lesson effectively.

Successful Gymnastics Teaching

The 1996 Ofsted Report (*Physical Education and Sport in Schools, a Survey of Good Practice*) highlights the following characteristics of good practice:

■ high-quality teaching
■ high expectations
■ high levels of achievement
■ effective curriculum organization and planning
■ good systems of assessment, recording and reporting
■ established routines for dress, behaviour and apparatus handling
■ equality of opportunity and high participation rates.

These characteristics are not always easy to achieve but should be what every teacher of gymnastics works towards achieving. Careful planning, good observation, thorough evaluation and enthusiasm make a firm basis from which to develop your gymnastics teaching (see Tables 2.2 and 2.3).

DANCE

Dance in the primary school curriculum is concerned with children controlling and combining basic actions to express feelings and ideas in response to stimuli. Some experience of dance forms from other times and places is also important.

The QCA document *Maintaining Breadth and Balance* outlines what most children should be able to do in dance at the ends of Key Stages 1 and 2.

Expectations

By the end of key stage 1 it is expected that most children will be able to:

In dance

- ■ show control and co-ordination in the basic actions of travelling, jumping, turning, gesture and stillness;
- ■ perform simple rhythmic patterns and use movement expressively to explore moods and feelings in response to stimuli including music.

By the end of key stage 2 it is expected that most children will be able to:

In dance

- ■ compose and combine basic actions by varying shape, size, direction, level, speed, tension and continuity;
- ■ express feelings, moods and ideas through movement in response to stimuli including music;
- ■ perform dances from different times and places.

(QCA, 1998)

Both gymnastics and dance focus on developing control of the body, flexibility and mobility but dance focuses especially on movement that expresses and evokes emotion. The basic actions of dance – travelling, jumping, turning, gesture and stillness – show marked similarities to the basic actions of gymnastics but the intention in dance is to use the body expressively, often to convey ideas or moods. Children need to be made increasingly aware that the way in which an action is performed is all important. For example, travelling lightly, suddenly or smoothly will offer different ideas and feelings to both dancers and observers. Children need be helped to respond to a variety of stimuli, and to learn how to respond rhythmically and how to develop their responses in order to create their own dances.

During the primary school years, the emphasis should be on the experience of dancing and making dances that are not too closely structured and are not always recalled or repeated in exactly the same way. Much of children's experience should consist of responding to stimuli that have been carefully chosen for their evocative qualities, for example, music, poetry or percussion instruments. Ideas for stimulating movement or dramatic response can often stem from aspects of class work or arise from natural happenings, such as a fall of snow or a windy day.

Starting Points for Creative Dance

Children need exciting starting points that will stimulate a great variety of spontaneous dance. Stimuli that are relevant to the children's ages, interests and experiences are the most effective. A wide variety of stimuli are available to teachers: stories, poetry, paintings, music of all kinds, everyday activities, natural forms, occupations, games and toys are all effective (see Study Sheet 9).

Teachers should expect a wide range of individual responses to the stimuli and should be prepared to 'feed in' ideas and teaching points to help everyone develop beyond their original response to the stimulus without taking away the individuality of each child's response.

Language

Spoken language has a huge role to play in helping the children to interpret and improve the expressive qualities of their actions. There are many words to describe travelling actions but they all require different movement responses and convey different ideas, moods and feelings, for example:

STAMP   GALLOP   TIPTOE   SKIP   STRIDE   MARCH   WALK

TROT   STEP   SCURRY   RUN   CREEP   SLITHER   SLIDE

Teachers need to become familiar with a wide range of descriptive words for use in creative dance. The list of descriptive words for dance actions in Figure 2.7 is very useful in developing children's movement responses.

These descriptive words can be made into phrases by teachers or children and offer useful stimuli for expressive movement. The way in which the voice is used should add clarity and further expression to the description. Consider your use of pitch, tone and volume.

Towards a Wider Vocabulary of Movement

Creative dance in primary education should develop children's ability to combine basic actions to express feelings, moods and ideas as well as to perform dances from other times and places. To be able to do this, children must have a wide movement vocabulary from which they can choose actions with which to plan their dances.

In dance it can be helpful to focus on four aspects of movement vocabulary: actions, dynamics, space and relationships. Table 2.4 gives some examples of what these four aspects might mean and how movements can be created by selecting examples from each aspect, for example:

Step quickly forwards towards my partner
Step gently backwards alone

RUN	JUMP	HOP	SKIP	ROLL
SLIDE	HOVER	SLITHER	GLIDE	WHISK
WHIRL	SHRINK	EXPAND	STRETCH	FREEZE
LEAP	BOUND	STRIDE	CURL	SQUEEZE
FALL	TWIRL	REVOLVE	POUNCE	FLOAT
DART	FLUTTER	WALK	STALK	RISE
COLLAPSE	STAMP	DODGE	JERK	FALL
BALANCE	DIVE	OPEN	CLOSE	WRIGGLE
PRESS	CREEP	SHAKE	GROW	
TWIST	TURN	STOP	SHRIVEL	GALLOP
TOSS	SWING	SPREAD	SWIRL	
TIPTOE	HIT	SHOOT	BOUNCE	ENCIRCLE
STEP	KICK	SHRUG	SPIN	CRAWL
LIFT	MELT SHATTER	DRIFT	SWAY	
ROCK	FLOP	PULL	PUSH	SHIVER
FLY	CROUCH	BURST	EXPLODE	SETTLE
ARCH	RUSH	TAP	TREMBLE	PAUSE
KNEEL	LIE	CRUMBLE	PLUNGE	ZIGZAG
DASH	SKIM	WHIP		
WANDER	FLICK	DAB	WRING	DRAG
	STAND	SCATTER		SOAR

FIGURE 2.7 Descriptive words for dance actions

high in the air–

and–

suddenly–

gently–

drift–

'explode–

to the

ground'

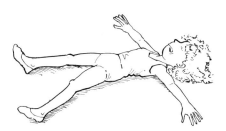

FIGURE 2.7 continued   Descriptive words for dance actions

Creating dances involves planning and performing appropriate movement vocabulary to express particular ideas, moods or feelings. In the early years, ideas and the choice of language will probably come from the teacher, for example:

ACTION	DYNAMICS	SPACE	RELATIONSHIP
Rolling ...	slowly ...	across the floor ...	towards the group
Leaping ...	powerfully ...	over ...	my partner

TABLE 2.4   Examples of the four aspects of dance movement vocabulary: actions, dynamics, space and relationships

Actions	Dynamics	Space	Relationship
'What do I do?'	'How do I do it?'	'Where do I do it?'	'With whom do I do it?'
Transferring weight: step, sit, kneel, rock, sway, flop, collapse, fall, handstand, cartwheel	Quickly, slowly, powerfully, gently, directly, wiggly, sharply, floppily, alertly, lazily	Forwards, backwards, sideways, straight, curved, zigzag, up, down, across, over, under, through, near, far, towards, away from, surround	Approach, meet, part, pass, with, against, lead, follow, question, answer, together, separately, alone, my partner, a group
Jumping: hop, leap, bounce			
Travelling: run, roll, slither, creep		Size: big, small	
Turning: spin, spiral, twirl, twist		Shape: curved, twisted, pointed	
Gesturing: stretch, reach, balance, wave, kick, nod, clap, pull, push, grab, hug, lean, slap			

With experience and a wider movement vocabulary, children will begin to develop their own ideas, language and appropriate actions.

As in gymnastics, children should be taught to adapt the basic actions of dance by varying body shape, directions, levels, and speed as well as considering size, tension and continuity. For instance, there are innumerable ways of travelling in the context of creative dance. A simple action, travelling, is not simple at all when used in conjunction with all the other aspects of dance.

Variations on the Basic Action of Travelling

Tables 2.5, 2.6 and 2.7 illustrate variations on the basic action of travelling.

Creative dance makes a unique contribution to the physical education curriculum with its focus on individual responses, personal expression and non-verbal communication. Traditional dance makes a different but still unique contribution to children's learning and development.

Traditional Dance

The QCA document (1998) *Maintaining Breadth and Balance* expects that by the end of Key Stage 2, most children are able to perform dances from different times and places.

TABLE 2.5   Changes in direction, level and pathway add variety to the basic action of travelling

Direction	Level	Pathway
Forwards	High	Straight
Backwards	Medium	Angular
Sideways, etc.	Low, etc.	Curved, etc.

TABLE 2.6   Changes in the manner of the action and the body parts used add variety to the basic action of travelling

Manner	Body parts
Strong	Two feet
Careful/Delicate	One foot and one hand
Heavy/Limp	Back
Fast	Side
Slow	Front
In sudden bursts	Hands and knees
Having stops	Two hands, one foot

TABLE 2.7   Changes in the travelling action and body shape add variety to the basic action of travelling

Body action in travelling	Body shape in travelling
Jump	Spread
Turn	Elongated
Rise	Curved
Sink	Contracted
Extended	Twisted
Shrink	Irregular/Symmetrical

Traditional dance can help children achieve this expectation, can be fun and is an excellent opportunity to integrate health-related fitness and exercise. It can develop:

wider movement vocabulary
steps and step patterns
poise, balance and coordination
movement memory
spatial awareness
historical context
social skills

planning, performing and evaluative skills
rhythm and phrasing
sequencing skills
creativity
partner and group work
many musical elements
communication skills

In the past, traditional dance has often been taught through the rules and regulations of country dancing, where children have been required to learn dances with very complex patterns and movements with very little previous experience, knowledge or understanding of the skills required. There has often been scarce evidence of progression and certainly few opportunities for children to plan or evaluate their work.

In teaching traditional dance, teachers should aim to gradually build up the children's skills and knowledge just like in any other area of the curriculum.

The following is adapted from *Up the Sides and Down the Middle* (Upton and Paine, 1996).

Basic Skills of Traditional Dance

In traditional dance, children need to learn about steps, spatial awareness, phrasing and relationships before complex established traditional dances can be tackled successfully.

Steps

Teach children to walk, jog, skip, gallop to the beat:

- keeping the same pulse and travelling at different speeds
- taking small steps or large steps, hopping, jumping on the spot or travelling
- using different parts of the foot, e.g. heel and toe
- encouraging children to make up their own steps.

Spatial awareness

Develop spatial awareness by walking, jogging, skipping, galloping:

- on the spot, around the room, in and out of others
- changing direction on command or on own initiative
- forwards, sideways or backwards
- in straight, curved, zigzag or figure-of-eight pathways.

Phrasing

Being able to 'feel' the phrasing of the music can be difficult and children need a great deal of experience of:

- going and stopping, on the spot or travelling
- responding to the phrasing of the music, clapping
- responding to phrasing by changing actions when the music changes, e.g. 8 bars walking, 8 bars stamping, etc.

Relationships

Working with partners or in small groups always offers challenges. This can be helped by children learning how to:

- make eye contact with partner where possible
- follow my leader, travelling in twos, threes, fours, etc.
- walk, skip and turn with a partner while holding hands
- travel towards or away or sideways while facing a partner,
- turn a partner and turn with a partner
- explore a variety of partner holds
- on a given signal make groups of two or three or four or five, etc.

Composition skills

Once children have some experience, knowledge and understanding of basic traditional dance skills, they can compose their own dances. They might give them names, record them in writing, diagrams or photographs and might teach them to other children.

In order to help children compose their own dances they need to be taught how to:

make their own patterns, e.g. claps, steps, stamps
combine actions and sequences, e.g.

    on the spot

in different pathways
using different movements (travel, turn, jump, etc.)

(Adapted from *Up the Sides and Down the Middle*, Upton and Paine, 1996)

Once children have experienced some of the basic skills, they are able to create their own folk dances and learn some of the simpler established traditional dances. In creating their own folk dances it is important to remember to:

- encourage innovation
- encourage experimentation
- ensure that what is created is dance and not gymnastics
- make the sections of the dance link smoothly from one section to another
- ensure the dance fits the music
- consider the creative inspiration for the dance and perhaps give it a related name.

When teachers are ready to teach some established traditional dances, there are many published resources, usually with accompanying music on cassette, from which to choose.

Lesson Planning in Dance

Whole-school or whole-Key-Stage schemes of work need breaking down into units of work, covering approximately half a term, and then into individual lesson plans. Beware of the tendency to try to cover too much in one lesson; children need time to experiment, practise and refine their movements. It is better to do only a little, well, than to rush through too much material. Be very focused in your teaching and learning objectives so that quality movement can be developed.

A dance lesson usually has four parts:

- a warm-up (2–3 minutes)
- development of main movement idea (8–10 minutes)
- the dance – individually, with a partners or in small groups (10–12 minutes)
- concluding activity (1–2 minutes).

The 'warm-up' part of the lesson should:

- warm the children physically
- start the lesson in a lively way
- accustom the children to the working environment

■ be an introduction to what follows.

The 'development' part of the lesson should include:

■ exploration of the main movement ideas
■ individual or very small group work
■ focus on awareness of the body, space, actions or dynamics.

The 'dance' part of the lesson should include:

■ linking the movements explored and developed earlier to create simple pieces of dance individually, with a partner or in small groups
■ dances with clear starting and finishing positions.

The 'concluding activity' may:

■ be a shared discussion about the lesson
■ be slow and gentle actions to calm the pupils down and to provide an orderly finish to the lesson
■ be used to discuss what has been learned or developed during the lesson
■ be used as a time to praise the children for their work.

Assessment in Dance

(See also Chapter 6 on Assessment Reporting and Recording.) Assessment in dance is primarily through teacher observation and as a non-specialist teacher of dance, assessment of the children's work can be difficult.

Columns (a) and (b) in Table 2.8 should help teachers to focus their observations and make some judgements about the children's progression and attainment. With a stimulating and progressive series of lessons, the qualities in column (a) should develop towards those in column (b).

It is important to encourage children to make judgements about their own and others' performance. Use your own observations and use of questioning to assist your assessments, encourage peer observation and promote learning.

Cross-curricular Links

Dance can easily be used to explore and enhance most primary school topic areas, to develop classroom work in another medium.

Specific ideas of how to link dance with other areas of the curriculum can be

TABLE 2.8   Assessing dance through teacher observation

(a) How you are likely to see the children moving to begin with	(b) How you hope to see the children moving
Moving the feet only	Moving with a change of weights using a variety of body parts
Dances with little structure	Dances with clear beginnings, middles and ends
Moving at the same level	Moving at a variety of changing levels
Moving at the same speed	Moving at a variety of speeds with acceleration and deceleration
Moving in an uninteresting way	Moving showing a variety of ideas
Lack of awareness of what other body parts are doing	Good body shape whilst moving and whilst still
Moving clumsily	Moving sensitively in relation to the floor space and to other children
Little expression of moods/feelings in response to stimulus	Greater expression of moods/feelings in response to stimulus
Little control of body tension, balance and stillness	Developing control of body tension, balance and stillness
Poor rhythmic responses	Developing rhythmic responses

found in any of the dance resources listed in the References and Further Reading lists at the end of the book. (See Study Sheet 10.)

Music for Dance

It is possible to use any music for dance, but some pieces are more suitable than others. Classical music is excellent, providing that it is not too complex. Choose pieces that either suggest one way of moving very clearly, for example:

Dukes' 'Sorcerer's Apprentices' (light and bouncy)
Brahms' 'Hungarian Dances' (fast and powerful)
Saint Saens' 'Swan' from 'Carnival of the Animals' (slow and gentle)

or have a very strong contrast, for example:

Richard Strauss's 'Also Sprach Zarahustr' (from *2001* soundtrack)
Copeland's 'Fanfare for the Common Man'

Grieg's 'Hall of the Mountain King'
Ravel's 'Bolero'.

These pieces build in intensity rather than contrast.

Music written in several movements, or as a suite, often has contrasts between the sections, as well as within them. For example:

Handel's 'Water Music'
Vivaldi's 'The Four Seasons'
Holst's 'The Planets'.

Music from shows and musicals is useful, for example:

Cats
42nd Street
Oliver
Annie
Bugsy Malone
Starlight Express.

Film music is written to reinforce a mood and is often an excellent resource for dance, for example:

Ennio Morricone (*The Good, The Bad and The Ugly, Once Upon a Time in the West*, etc.)
Mike Oldfield (*The Killing Fields*)
John Carpenter (*Halloween, Escape from New York*, etc.).

Compilations of TV and radio themes are also very useful. Children enjoy working with music they recognize. Beware of using any music with lyrics!

Look through your own music collection and that of your friends and family. You may be surprised at how many instrumental pieces there are that you could use for dance.

SWIMMING

Individual schools will have very differing policies for the teaching of swimming for a number of reasons. Pool provision is an obvious consideration with some schools having their own pool on site or within walking distance whilst some schools, in outlying areas, may have very long coach journeys to reach their nearest pool.

Schools that have to travel a long way to reach a swimming pool are unlikely to have policies that include swimming for all Key Stage 2 or for any Key Stage 1 children because it would be too costly in terms of time and money. Swimming pools are very expensive to maintain, even for one term each year, and any on-site provision needs to be used extensively in order to justify the financial cost. Schools with their own pools will often have policies which include swimming for all children for up to five times each week. This is clearly very expensive in terms of time and often other areas of the physical education curriculum can be neglected.

The recent introduction of the 'Literacy Hour' and the forthcoming introduction of the 'Numeracy Hour' has increased the pressures on time within the primary school day and has led to schools being given more flexibility about how much of the National Curriculum foundation subjects needs to be retained. The QCA document *Maintaining Breadth and Balance* (1998) outlines the new flexible arrangements for the National Curriculum in foundation subjects at Key Stages 1 and 2, but there is no flexibility for swimming. The document clearly states that:

Swimming remains a statutory requirement at key stage 2.

You may choose to teach swimming in key stage 1 using the key stage 2 programme of study set out in the National Curriculum Order for physical education.

(QCA 1998)

National Curriculum for Physical Education: Programme of Study for Swimming in Key Stage 1 and/or 2

a   to swim unaided, competently and safely, for at least 25 metres;
b   to develop confidence in water, and how to rest, float and adopt support positions;
c   a variety of means of propulsion using either arms or legs or both, and how to develop effective and efficient swimming strokes on the front and the back;
d   the principles and skills of water safety and survival.

(DFE 1995)

The fact that swimming is the only area of any foundation subject that has remained statutory and for which the full programme of study from the National Curriculum Orders for Physical Education is still to be taught, reflects its importance.

Organization, Management and Safety in Swimming

In any class of children there are likely to be greater differences in individuals' experience and abilities in swimming than in any other area of the entire curriculum. Some children will have had private swimming lessons and may even be being coached to swim for their county, whilst other children may have never been to a swimming pool in their lives. Clearly these differences will need to be taken into account when planning swimming lessons and it is most usual for swimming to be taught in ability groups with some schools linking classes together so that children can be grouped across more than one class.

Teachers should never rely on 'hearsay' evidence of children's swimming ability. A friend of mine had a new child join her class midway through the term. The child's swimming costume was festooned with swimming badges and my friend assumed she was quite competent in the water. Unfortunately, the costume had come from a jumble sale, complete with badges and the child had never been swimming in her life! If there are no previous records of children's swimming abilities, then teachers should spend the first lesson making judgements about individuals as they show what they can do in the water, starting with activities for beginners in shallow water, then moving onto swimming activities in shallow water before entering deep water.

It is usual to divide swimming lessons into at least three ability groups to cater for weak or non-swimmers, those able to manage a few widths and those of advanced ability. In large public pools, some swimming teaching is often available from the pool staff, thus allowing for more than one group to be easily taught at the same time. In smaller 'on-site' pools, teachers often have to use quite a complex 'circus'-type of organization, where they work with one group in the water whilst other groups are dressing or undressing under the supervision of support staff or parent helpers.

There are many factors to consider when taking children swimming and it is essential that the children are familiar with the procedures before the lesson, whether using a public pool or an on-site school pool. Safety and learning rely on good organization and management.

- Divide children into ability groups, usually non-swimmers, beginners and swimmers.
- How you organize swimming time will depend upon the space available and the number of supervising adults.
- Check on the swimming ability of all children and don't believe everything they tell you!
- Make sure you know how many children are in the group – do regular counts.
- Check that all children can hear and see you during the giving of instructions both on the way to the pool, on the pool side and in the water.
- Clearly define the working area within the pool, perhaps by using ropes.
- Keep non-swimmers within their depth by the use of roped-off areas as necessary.

- Have all the equipment ready at the side of the pool.
- Have clear starting and stopping signals.
- A whistle is essential for use in emergencies.

Safety

- Never leave children unsupervised, either in the water or on the pool side.
- If you are in charge of the children, you should never go into the water except in cases of emergency.
- Ensure you keep all the children in the water in your vision at all times.
- Ensure you are familiar with the pool depths, etc.
- Make children aware of safety factors before they go into the water.
- Be aware of procedures in case of any accident.
- Check on rules at the pool for medical, safety and hygiene issues.
- Ensure good discipline and quick responses to instructions.
- Encourage safe entry and exit from the water.
- Keep the noise level down.
- Consider the safety factors affecting the journey to and from the pool, and during the changing routine.
- Check the group for medical problems in advance of the lesson.

Whilst careful planning, good organization and appropriate risk assessment will maximize safety, there are many issues related to specific environments and situations that will need consideration. Teachers need to familiarize themselves with their own school's swimming routines and environment.

Lesson Planning in Swimming

Units of work for swimming could be developed during Key Stage 1 or Key Stage 2 or in both key stages and should include the aspects listed below:

- Work for beginners and non-swimmers, going in and coming out of the pool, moving in water, activities to keep feet off the bottom, submerging, an introduction to breathing in water, driving the body through water, floating and support positions.
- Stroke development, gliding, strokes on front and back.
- Elementary survival skills, to be covered in the normal teaching programmes.
- Water safety, principles and skills, dangers in and around water, actions required in emergency situations, helping others, knowing the importance of swimming and water safety skills in supporting other water-based activities and activities near water.

■ Simple games, walking races, treading-water contest, follow the leader, picking up objects from the bottom, relays, ball games including aiming at targets, small-sided versions of water polo.

Units of work will need to take account of the varying abilities within a class. Separate plans will probably need to be written for at least three levels or ability groups: beginners, those who are just able to swim and strong swimmers.

Even though group work is likely to be the most usual teaching strategy, the lesson for each group should contain warm-up activities, some development of strokes and other skills and a concluding activity. During a 40-minute swimming session, some groups may only be in the water for 10 minutes, so it is important that they are active for as much of that time as possible.

Activities for Beginnings and Ends of Swimming Lessons

Warm-up or introductory activities:

should be active
should be enjoyable
should help the children get used to the water temperature
should establish class control, organization and spacing
should establish concentration
should be familiar yet interesting
should contrast with the main stroke-technique session.

Concluding activities:

should be challenging
should be enjoyable
should contrast with the stroke-technique sessions
should occasionally offer opportunities for personal practice
should sometimes introduce new ideas.

Warm-up activities for beginners need to build confidence whilst those for other swimmers might include floating, gliding, under water experiences, simple synchronized swimming activities, endurance activities, speed work and activities that focus on life-saving skills.

Suggested Warm-up Activities for Beginners:

- holding the rail, jumping up and down, bringing shoulders under the water
- holding onto the rail floating on one's front and beating the legs up and down
- holding the rail, floating on one's back, beating the legs up and down
- walking away from rail, turning and walking back, keeping the shoulders under the water
- jumping away from rail, keeping the arms outstretched for balance, turning and jumping back to the rail
- jumping and splashing the arms to wet the face
- moving along with the chin on the surface of the water, blowing a light-weight ball or rubber duck in front of the mouth
- playing 'Simon says'
- playing follow my leader, in twos or threes.

Suggested Warm-up Activities for Non-beginners:

Floating and gliding

- pushing off from the side of the pool on one's front and gliding, noting the distance travelled
- pushing and gliding even further
- pushing and gliding, then floating in a star shape
- performing mushroom floats, long floats, and front, back and side floats
- floating, rolling over back to front through the vertical and horizontal axes.

Under water

- touching the bottom of the pool with the foot, hand, seat or knee
- swimming under water and noting the distance
- swimming through a hoop
- doing handstands
- doing surface dives
- picking up a rubber brick
- swimming down to touch line on bottom of pool.

Synchronized swimming activities

- sculling – on back, on front, feet first, head first
- devising partner sequences

■ devising floating shapes.

Endurance

■ swimming for 20 seconds without stopping
■ swimming x widths or part widths without stopping
■ swimming and resting – measured distance, timed rest.

Speed

■ timing how many seconds it takes to swim x widths
■ trying again – but trying to swim faster
■ measuring how far one can swim in x seconds.

Life-saving activities

■ life saving a float, i.e. holding the float above the water and swimming across the pool
■ holding a float above water and doing back stroke across the pool
■ practising a life-saving leg kick, i.e. an inverted breast-stroke leg kick
■ walking while towing a partner held in a life-saving hold, i.e. under the chin
■ practising RLSS Water Safety Award activities
■ learning about cardiac pulmonary resuscitation.

Competitive activities   (for personal challenge, or against others)

■ finding out how quickly, for example, two lines at the bottom of the pool can be touched with the hand; touching one line and jumping over the second
■ holding the rail and finding out who can do 20 kicks fastest
■ trying to tread water for 2 minutes
■ finding out who is the first to jump 10 times and clap their hands under water 10 times.

Water polo activities

■ passing a ball in pairs or in small groups
■ playing water volley ball, i.e. keeping a light ball in the air individually or in pairs
■ swimming to pick up the ball
■ practising aiming the ball.

Stroke development should follow the warm-up part of the lesson. When working with beginners, the emphasis should be on fun and building confidence in the water before trying formally to teach them to swim.

Progressive Ideas for Building Beginners' Confidence

Entry into the Water

This can be the most frightening part of the lesson and needs to be carefully considered. The following activities can help build a child's confidence.

- walking backwards down the steps 'like firemen down their ladders'
- sitting on the side of the pool, putting both hands palms down on one side of the body, swivelling and lowering the body into the water
- jumping into the pool from a crouching position
- jumping into the pool from a standing position.

Movement

It is important to get beginners moving as soon as they get into the water or they will become very cold very quickly. The following activities can be practised.

- holding the rail and walking (varying the size of steps and the direction of steps)
- holding the rail and jumping up and down with the shoulders going under the water
- walking away from the rail, turning and walking back
- walking in a space with the chin on the water, using long steps with the arms spread out on the surface of the water for balance
- walking along holding bar, or walking in a space using big steps, little steps, turning steps, and moving quickly or slowly
- clapping while moving
- holding hopping, skipping, jumping, wriggling
- jumping and splashing water to wet the face
- moving while singing simple songs or nursery rhymes, for example, 'We All Live in a Yellow Submarine', 'Five little Ducks', '1, 2, 3, 4, 5, Once I caught a fish alive'.

Flotation

A relaxed body is more likely to float than a tense body. Children tend to hold their breath, so asking them to smile broadly at you often makes them exhale and consequently relax. The following can be practised to help the body relax and float.

- holding sitting low-down in the water, shoulders submerged and gently raising the bent knees to stand up
- facing and holding the rail, straightening the arms, lying down and kicking the legs up behind
- lying on the water, holding rail and making big splashes or small splashes
- sitting in the water, moving the legs out behind to lie on the water, then standing up
- sitting in the water, moving the legs out in front to lie on the back and then standing up
- floating, sitting, lying on the front or back, making a long shape, a star shape, a curved shape or a tucked shape.

Propulsion

Propulsion means moving through the water in any way. For example:

- holding sitting in the water, arms stretched out widely on the water, bringing the knees up and paddling the toes – moving forwards or backwards
- sitting in the water, paddling with the hands, then moving in a circle, back the other way, then forwards, then backwards
- sitting in the water with the shoulders submerged, then lifting up the tummy, lying on the back and kicking the toes
- as above, but lifting up the back to lie on the front and then kicking the toes
- experiment with movements in the water while holding a float.

Submerging

Some children really hate getting water in their faces but activities that do this in a controlled way can build their confidence.

- holding blowing bubbles on surface of water, lifting the head, breathing in and blowing again
- drawing shapes on the water with the nose
- holding the rail, kicking the legs and blowing bubbles. Finding out how noisy this can be!

- blowing a light-weight ball or plastic duck across pool when walking or swimming
- taking three high jumps and bobbing down low in the water
- bobbing down in the water to touch the toes
- bobbing down in the water to touch a line at the bottom of the pool
- sitting on the bottom of pool
- kneeling on the bottom of pool
- bobbing down and picking up a rubber brick from the bottom of the pool
- pushing from the side, gliding on the front, face down
- bobbing down, creeping along under the water and popping up in a new place
- singing 'Ring O' Ring O' Roses' with actions!

Once beginners have gained some confidence in the water, formal swimming strokes can be introduced.

Swimming Strokes

It is important that children have the opportunity to try out all the swimming strokes, especially when they are beginners. Many children learn to swim through a variation of front crawl (doggy-paddle style) but some learn breast stroke first and others prefer to swim on their backs.

All swimming strokes are made up of five aspects:

body position
leg action
arm action
timing
breathing.

When observing children who can swim but do not seem to be moving efficiently and easily through the water, close observation of each of these aspects will usually indicate where further teaching is required.

Detailed analyses of each aspect of the three most common strokes, breaststroke, front crawl and back crawl, are listed below. These can be used as foci for observation and teaching points, as teaching and learning objectives when planning units of work, as individual lessons and as assessment criteria.

The Breast Stroke

Body position

- The body lies in the water as flat as possible and the legs bend at the knees.

The feet will come out of the water during the leg kick if the hips are too high.

■ Eyes look forward at a point just below the surface of the water. Chin rests on the surface of the water throughout the stroke. Hips come just below the surface.

■ Feet finish leg kick (propulsive phase) about 20 cm below the surface.

Leg action   Put simply, the heels draw symmetrical circles just below the surface of the water.

■ The legs start together in a stretched (extended) position.
■ The heels are drawn up towards the seat by bending (flexing) the knees, with the knees slightly apart.
■ The feet turn outwards with the soles of the feet facing uppermost, just below the surface of the water. It can be useful to describe this to children as 'Charlie Chaplin' or 'Frog Feet' and to demonstrate it in a standing position on the pool side.
■ The kick is made symmetrically in an outwards and backwards action. Some children will seem to be kicking in an asymmetrical way. This is usually caused by either twisting the body or kicking more strongly with one leg than the other.
■ The legs reach full stretch (extension) ready to begin the next kick.

Arm action   Put simply; the hands draw symmetrical circles in front of the face just under the surface of the water.

■ The arms commence and finish the movement at full stretch, with the hands touching, the little fingers slightly raised and about 15–20 cm below the surface.
■ The wrists flex and tend to turn outwards as each arm moves in a sideways direction.
■ The fingers of each hand should be kept together so that more 'pull' through the water is achieved.
■ The arms, during the sideways movement, press slightly downwards, when the hands are about body width apart.
■ The wrists and forearms accelerate in a movement back to the centre.
■ When the hands are almost touching, the elbows come in towards each other and the hands are pushed forwards to full stretch.

Timing

■ First, the arms pull and the legs remain straight.

- The arms recover and the legs begin to bend.
- The arms push forward and the legs begin to kick back.
- The arms are at full stretch, the legs finish with a backwards kick.

Breathing   Breathing is rarely a problem in breast stroke as the face is out of the water but the teaching points below can help the smooth flow of the stroke.

- Inhalation usually takes place towards the end of the pulling action of the arms. The pulling-down action lifts the shoulders and head, facilitating breathing.
- Exhalation takes place as the arms are pushed forwards near full stretch.

The Front Crawl

Body position   In order to be able to swim front crawl efficiently, children need to be comfortable with their faces in the water.

- The body is flat and extended.
- The eyes look forward through the water to a point 15cm deep and about an arm's length in front of the face.
- The water meets the face at the hair line.
- The hips are approximately 3–4 cm below the surface.
- The feet alternate upwards towards the surface.

Leg action   Put simply, the legs are straight and work in a scissor action up and down.

- The body position is horizontal, extended and flat.
- The back and legs are just beneath surface and not too steeply inclined.
- The heels should just break the surface of the water on the up kick.
- The depth of kick is approximately 30–45 cm.
- The legs should be extended, though not rigid, with the toes pointing away from the body.
- The kick originates from the hip and travels down through the leg to the foot.
- The knees bend just a little.
- The legs kick alternatively and continuously.

Arm action   Put simply, the arms make a large, alternate windmill action.

- The arm extends forward from the shoulders – a natural arm's reach.
- The fingers slide into the water – no splash.

- The fingers should be kept tightly together to give more pull through the water.
- The arm cycle is in three parts – pull down – push back – recovery.
- The 'pull-down' and 'push-back' phrases are beneath the surface of the water.
- The 'recovery' phase takes place above the surface of the water.
- The arm enters the water in the order of – hand, wrist, forearm, elbow.
- The hand moves at sufficient speed to generate propulsion.
- The hand emerges from the water close to the hip.
- The arm is lifted from water, with the elbow leading.
- The recovery is effected by bringing the hands and arms over the head, clear of the water.

Breathing   Breathing in the front crawl requires children to be comfortable with their faces under the water and can be difficult to coordinate.

- A regular breathing pattern must be established.
- Breathing can take place with the head on either side.
- Inhalation takes place as the arm commences recovery.
- Exhalation takes place under the water through mouth and nose.
- The head faces the front during exhalation.
- The angle of the head positions the hairline on the water line.
- The swimmer may breathe in on same side at every stroke (unilateral breathing).
- The swimmer may breathe in on alternate sides every 1.5 strokes (bilateral breathing).

Coordination

- The leg action counterbalances the arm action.
- Tenseness tends to create 'rolling' from the shoulders and then the whole body.
- The rhythm of complete strokes should be smooth and flowing.

The Back Crawl

Position of body

- Throughout the stroke the body remains straight.
- The body position is horizontal, extended and almost flat on the surface of the water.
- The chest and head are level with the surface of water.

■ Hips are required to be just beneath the water, avoiding sinking of the seat and 'sitting' in the water.
■ The angle of the head is slightly forward, eyes looking at a point above the hips. If the head is lifted up, the hips will tend to sink.

Leg action　Put simply, the legs are straight and work in a scissor action, up and down.

■ The legs stay close together and kick alternately.
■ Leg action originates from the hips and travels down through the legs to the ankles and feet.
■ The legs should be extended, though not rigid, with the toes pointing away from body.
■ Maintaining flexible ankles gives more power to the kick.

Arm action　Put simply, the arms make a large, alternate windmill action.

■ The arm cycle is in three parts – pull, push and recovery.
■ The 'pull' and 'push' phases are beneath the water.
■ The 'recovery' phase takes place above the water.
■ The arm reaches behind the shoulder, a natural arm's reach.
■ The point of entry into water is in front of and directly in line with the shoulder, the hand enters the water, little finger first.
■ The 'push' continues to approximately level with the waist.
■ The hand leaves the water in a vertical line, index finger first, the arm fully extended, the elbow straight, the wrist relaxed.

Coordination

■ The action of the legs counterbalances the rolling action of the arms.
■ The rapid kicking of legs is often '6 beats' to a complete arm action.
■ Breathing should not create any difficulties.

Table 2.9 shows a range of swimming skills, the reasons for teaching these skills and appropriate teaching points for developing the skills.

TABLE 2.9 A range of swimming skills, the reason for teaching these skills and appropriate points for developing these skills

Skills: 1	Teaching points
1 Push and glide on front	Stretch body. Face in water. Eyes looking towards bottom of pool. Legs straight and together. Toes pointed
2 Push and glide on back	Stretch body. Tummy and hips high in water. Eyes looking upwards. Legs straight and together. Toes pointed
3 Star-float on front	Arms stretched out beyond head. Legs apart. Relax. Face in water. Eyes looking downwards
4 Star-float on back	Arms stretched out beyond head. Legs apart. Relax. Head and ears in water. Eyes looking upwards
5 Pick up an object from bottom of pool using *both* hands	Object placed in front of swimmer. Big breath in. Jump up, bend legs. Place both hands on object and retrieve
6 5-metre swim on front change to 5-metre swim on back without putting feet down	Smooth transition from front to back. Keep legs kicking as body rolls over to back. Keep body moving forward
7 5-metre swim on back change to 5-metre swim on front without putting feet down	Smooth transition from back to front. Keep legs kicking as body rolls over to front. Keep body moving forward
8 Mushroom float for 5 seconds	Big breath in. Slowly tuck legs under body. Hands placed around lower legs. Chin on chest. Face in water. Breathe out slowly
9 Bob down, push and glide	Straight back as body goes under water. Bend legs. Place feet on wall. Give strong push off. Stretch body. Point fingers up to glide to surface. Legs straight

Reason

Streamlining of body position for swimming and diving.
Early confidence practice.

Streamlining of body position for swimming and diving.
Body position for floating

Confidence practice
Practice for using natural buoyancy

Confidence practice. Feeling of stretching body
Practice for using natural buoyancy

Picking up object with both hands ensures face goes under the water
Aquatic confidence for swimming and diving

Body awareness. Gives confidence
Can be used in case of an emergency

Body awareness. Confidence practice

Beginning of aquatic breathing.
Practice for using natural buoyancy

Initial practice for the under-water section of diving and turns

TABLE 2.9 *Continued*

Skills: 2	Teaching points
1 Handstands	Big breath in. Chin on chest. Bend at waist. Pull arms sideways to pull top half of body forwards/downwards. Place hands flat on pool bottom. Arch back to keep legs in line and above body
2 Swim through partner's legs	Big breath in. Chin on chest. Bend at waist. Use breast-stroke arm action. Pull back to side of body. Keep head lower than body to help gain and maintain depth. Tilt hands up to come to surface
3 Head-first surface dive, swim 5metres underwater	As above
4 Breast stroke, legs (holding floats either two floats, one in each hand, arms apart, or one float held by two hands, arms stretched out in front of face.	Heels up to seat, hip width apart. Feet turn out. Draw circles with feet. Legs drive backwards. Finish with straight legs together. Toes pointed
5 Front crawl, legs (with a float held by two hands, arms stretched out in front of face)	Kick from hips. Straight legs. Legs move up and down as close together as possible. Stretch ankles and feet
6 Back crawl, legs (with float held by both hands either on tummy or with arms stretched out above head)	Look up. Tummy and hips up. Straight legs. Kick from hips. Legs close together. Stretch feet and ankles. Point toes. Flick water away. Toes just come to water surface
7 H.E.L.P. (*HEAT ESCAPE LESSENING POSTURE*) position for 2 minutes, holding a floating object	Keep arms tight against sides of body, while holding a floating object. Lie on back. Bend legs up towards body
8 10-metre swim on front	Front crawl or breast stroke demonstrating a good technique
9 10-metre swim on back	Back crawl, or inverted breast stroke demonstrating a good technique

Reason

Gives body awareness
Early practice for diving

Gives body awareness
Early practice for turns

Might be needed in an emergency situation

Early practice for correct leg and foot action, i.e no screw kick

Early practice for correct leg action

Early practice for correct leg action to balance arm action

Used as a survival position to protect areas of body that lose the most heat when immersed in cold water

Progress can be seen

Progress can be seen

OUTDOOR AND ADVENTUROUS ACTIVITIES

The QCA document *Maintaining Breadth and Balance* (1998) states that by the end of Key Stage 2, most children should be able to 'perform activities of a physical and problem-solving nature'. Whilst these aims are clearly important, outdoor and adventurous activities can contribute far more widely to children's education.

Outdoor and adventurous activities provide opportunities for children to participate in challenging situations within their school grounds, or sometimes off site, and which sometimes have an element of risk taking. The activities should not only present mental and physical challenges, but encourage children to work together cooperatively, building on trust and developing skills to solve problems either individually or as a member of a group. They must be given a sense of purpose and challenge and from this should come enjoyment and satisfaction from achieving the task.

Teachers need to appreciate that in outdoor and adventurous activities the learning processes are essentially practical, enquiry-based and pupil-orientated and that there is always potential for personal and social development.

The Aims of Outdoor and Adventurous Activities

- to provide children with challenges of a problem-solving nature, which bring about confidence, satisfaction and success
- to introduce children to different environments
- to explore other areas of the curriculum through the medium of outdoor activities
- to give children strategies for developing personal skills and interests
- to give children the opportunity to learn through fun activities
- to develop positive attitudes in children
- to build upon qualities of sharing, working together and developing ways of communicating
- to give opportunities to develop leadership skills.

Planning and Resourcing for Outdoor and Adventurous Activities

The initial preparation and research of resources for use in outdoor and adventurous activities can seem lengthy but once the resources are prepared, they are likely to be used in a variety of curriculum contexts.

Useful Resources

- Maps can be bought quite cheaply and it is well worth having them laminated to make them more durable. Simple teacher-drawn maps of the school and grounds and local area or plans of the school are excellent resources for outdoor and adventurous activities.
- It is useful to have a sufficient number of clipboards (non-cardboard), which make writing easier outside.
- Equipment such as milk crates, long ropes and drainpipes, although not standard in schools are very useful. These can usually be obtained free of charge or at a small cost from, for example, the local dairy, a builders merchant or parents. It can be very surprising what some parents have easy access to!
- Large balls of string and markers of many kinds are invaluable.
- Enough blindfolds are necessary for one between two. These can be easily made by a helpful parent using rectangles of dark fabric and elastic.
- A parachute (available from schools' suppliers) is useful. They are available in 2.5–30 metres in diameter, but one measuring 6–8 metres in diameter is suitable for primary school use. They fold down into small bags for easy storage.
- It is useful to have good-quality compasses, preferably enough for one between two. Ensure that compasses are not stored near anything made of metal.

Managing Resources

Ideally the children should be taught to set out courses and to carry and place equipment appropriately. If the whole school is involved, then it is possible that some equipment and courses could remain in place for the day and used by a number of classes.

Lesson Planning for Outdoor and Adventurous Activities

Although outdoor and adventurous activities are not likely to be areas of activity that take place every week of the school year, the children's learning still needs to be planned carefully. Some schools concentrate their outdoor and adventurous teaching into part of the summer term when some of the activities might take place in off-site camps or in other residential settings. No matter what amount of time is allocated, an overall picture of the school's policies and plans is necessary to ensure continuing challenge and progression. Teaching and learning objectives need to be clear in units of work and in individual lesson plans.

In deciding which activities to plan, many issues will need to be taken into account. What level of problem solving skills are you expecting the children to have? How fit are the children in your class? Are you wanting to provide opportunities for children to work together in small groups with the specific aim of developing cooperative skills or are you planning an appropriate activity to develop the communication skills of particular children?

As in all areas of activity in physical education, there are many opportunities for children to plan, perform and evaluate. They need to have time to plan and talk about the challenge that has been set, to do it and then possibly repeat it, or at least discuss it, in the light of their experiences.

Initially children may well find working together and trusting each other difficult but with carefully planned and progressive activities, not only will they gain directly from their outdoor and adventurous activities but many of the outcomes may benefit them in other areas of the curriculum and their school life.

Safety

Safety is, as ever in physical education, a high priority. With the use of some unorthodox equipment and perhaps playground and gymnastics apparatus, children need to be taught about its use within the context of outdoor and adventurous activities. For example, milk crates should be covered with a sheet of hardboard to prevent children's feet becoming stuck in the holes. Canes should always be carried upright and all equipment returned to base when not in use.

Children need to know the boundaries for trails and courses. If they are working in a public area, they should work in groups of not less than three and be taught what they should do if a problem arises.

Children need to be dressed appropriately for the activities. Track suit bottoms/leggings are best if they are exploring undergrowth or in woodland areas whilst T-shirts and shorts are best if water is involved in the activity. Boots or wellingtons may be the best footwear for some activities, trainers for others.

Outdoor and adventurous activities can be divided into four areas; problem solving, cooperation, trust and orienteering-type activities.

Problem-solving Activities

Problem-solving activities allow children to discuss their ideas freely and work together to achieve a successful solution. There are many others and all can be developed further.

Bench ordering: eight to ten children standing on a gymnastics bench   Children have to rearrange themselves without getting off, in order of height, birthday, alphabet, etc.

Circle knot: in groups of 10   Standing in a circle, each child extends his/her left hand and grasps someone else's hand across the circle. Keeping hold, this is repeated with the right hand. The children should try to unravel the knot without letting go and aim to end up in a circle again.

Fox, farmer duck and goose: in groups of four, each child wearing a band of one of three different colours   The 'farmer' has to take his animals over the river. They all start on the same side of the river. The 'birds' must not be left alone with the 'fox'. The farmer can take only one creature at a time in his boat.

Letter Game: children work in pairs   A word is used in which no two letters are the same, e.g. marigold, hamster. The word is cut up and the letters hidden or stuck up around the room or course. The children are divided into groups or pairs and are told how many letters to collect and that no two letters are the same. There should be enough cut-up words for each group/pair. The first group or pair to find the letters and reassemble the word scores points, etc. To make it more challenging, a time limit can be given.

Squares: children work in small groups (twos or threes)   Old birthday cards, Christmas cards, or postcards can be cut up into pieces. The pieces of the pictures are hidden by the teacher and each group has to reassemble its own picture.

Cooperative Activities

Cooperative activities bring together groups of children working towards a common aim.

Parachute Activities

These activities are excellent for developing cooperative skills with a whole class all participating together. To achieve anything with the parachute everyone has to work together and players need to be constantly aware of one another. Parachute activities can develop cooperation, fitness, coordination, awareness of space, observation, rhythm and listening skills to name but a few benefits. The activities can be very tiring but are also exhilarating. For many children working with a parachute may be a new experience and it is likely to create great excitement. Teacher needs to set their own rules for safety and have strong stop signals.

There are many parachute games and it is easy to adapt or develop your own, but a few examples are given below.

'Sway a day'   The children stand facing the parachute, holding it with both hands. They move their hands and arms rhythmically from left to right. By keeping the rhythm steady, but altering the height of their arms and bodies, a variety of effects can be achieved.

'Mexican wave'   The children stand and hold the parachute as in the previous activity, but one child in the circle starts off crouched down and the child opposite stretches up as high as possible with all the other children at various stages of crouching or standing in between. The aim is to move the high/low points around the circle by gradually bobbing up and down and creating a 'Mexican wave'.

'Mushrooms'   All the children to crouch around the parachute. At a given command, they stretch their arms high to lift the parachute. They then pull it down and lift it up repeatedly and rhythmically three or five times. On the third or fifth time, they pull the edges of the parachute to the floor quickly in order to trap air and create a 'mushroom'.

'Crossovers'   All the children stand around the parachute with their hands at chest height, rippling the parachute gently. At a given command, certain children let go and cross under the parachute to a new position, for example:

- 'Everyone in the red group, change places.'
- 'All those with birthdays in June, change places.'
- 'All those with two vowels in their surnames, change places.'
- 'All those whose age is an even number, change places.'

'Basketweave'   Standing around the parachute as in the previous activity, each child is given the number 1 or 2 alternatively around the parachute. The 1s ripple the parachute and the 2s weave in and out of the 1s in a clockwise direction until they return to their original position.

'Using balls and beanbags'   Place a large soft ball on the parachute and ask the children to:

- keep the ball moving, or
- roll it clockwise or

- roll it anticlockwise or
- toss the ball or beanbag into the air off the parachute and catch it again.

Other Cooperative Activites

Water pipe filling   On a hot day this is a wonderful activity! Children will need spare clothes and towels. The equipment needed consists of:

- water
- paper or plastic cups
- a piece of thin drain pipe with finger holes drilled into it, recorder style, and held vertically by two children
- a container from a camera film containing a message and placed in the bottom of the drainpipe
- 8/10 people per group (depending on the number of holes in the pipe).

The objective is to work together as a group to fill the water pipe and retrieve the message. The pipe needs to be well away from the water supply. The group needs to decide who is going to cover the holes and who is going to pour the water into the pipe. Speed is essential and the group needs to work together if they are going to be successful.

River crossing   The equipment needed consists of three milk crates and two long ropes. There should be five/six people per team.

The objective is for the whole team to cross the river by means of the crates without falling in! The two ropes are used to represent the 'river bank'. The crates are stacked up on one side of the bank beside the team and must be placed like stepping stones and not thrown across the 'river'. More than one team member can go across at a time.

Minefield   The equipment needed consists of two long ropes, a bucket and a hoop. The children are divided into groups of four. The children in each group are arranged in pairs opposite one another. Each child of the pair holds an end of one long rope, with their feet behind a marker (or line). Their task is to work together to use the two ropes to lift the bucket, which has been placed in the middle of the area into the hoop. The rope must not be tucked under the lip of the bucket nor must the children touch the bucket with their hands. To make the activity more difficult, some balls or water can be placed in the bucket!

It is often fun to set the following activities in context. For example, the group has set out on an adventure into the wild. They get lost, the weather changes and they need to make the following to keep warm, safe and dry!

Designing and making a wind gauge   The aim is to test the strength and direction of the wind. Equipment needed consists of string, glue, stick, card, paper, scissors and paper clips. Organization: working in small groups with sufficient materials for everyone.

Constructing a shelter   The aim is to house the whole group. Equipment needed consists of bin liners, string, canes, sellotape and scissors. Organization: working in groups of four/five, using available materials.

Each group is allowed two bin bags. Shelters can be free standing or attached to permanent structures or bushes. It is important to stress the need for resourcefulness. Extra points could be given for the sensitive use of natural materials!

Trust Activities

Over a period of time, trust activities develop personal and social skills and for some children this element is quite difficult as it involves working closely together with others or being dependent on a few. These activities work most successfully when you know your class well. Many of the activities listed below involve being blindfolded therefore safety implications need to be fully discussed and some rules laid down.

Activities Using a Blindfold

- In pairs, one child physically leads the blindfolded partner around the school hall or a designated area of the school either indoors or outside.
- In pairs, one child leads the blindfolded partner around a designated space by means of verbal instructions. This activity can be developed by placing obstacles in the space, e.g. chairs, ramps, gymnastic benches, etc. Once experienced, the leader can create a story about the obstacles, developing a directional vocabulary ('over', 'around', 'under', 'through', etc.). The story might be set in a jungle, in a busy town or on the moon! **Safety point**: children must never, whilst blindfolded, jump down from an obstacle.
- In pairs, one child leads the blindfolded partner outside to a string trail and leaves him/her to follow the route of the string. Objects to feel and remember can be hung from the string.
- **'Blindfold square'** requires eight blindfolded people and a long rope with the ends tied to form a continuous loop. The group is given the rope to hold and instructed to arrange themselves into a square within the confines of the loop.
- **'Water blindfold'** requires the blindfolded partner of a pair to thread a

piece of string through the handle of a mug of water. The string is extended along a designated area. His/her partner leads the blindfolded child around the course. The blindfolded person has to thread the mug of water along the string trying not to spill any of the water.

Other Activities

- In groups of six or seven, a tight circle is formed with one person in the middle. The person in the centre stands with his/her feet planted firmly on the ground with the arms folded across the chest and leans against the support offered by those in the circle. As confidence, skill and experience develops, the circle can become wider.
- Groups of 10–15 people form a very tight circle, with each child standing closely behind the person in front. At a given command, everyone bends their knees and 'sits' on the lap of the person behind. This can result in a surprisingly stable structure!

Orienteering Activities

Early orienteering and map work skills should begin in the classroom or hall by, for example, drawing a simple plan of the classroom to show the main features or drawing simple routes between different parts of the room.

Map Orientation

This activity requires each child to have paper, pencil and a clipboard.

- Four or five pieces of apparatus are placed in the hall and the children are asked to draw an outline plan or map of the hall, marking North, and drawing the apparatus on their plan. Symbols can be used to represent the apparatus. The children are then required to draw a line on their map that snakes around, under, over and through the apparatus. They are then asked to walk the route drawn on the map, keeping it pointing towards North. The maps can be exchanged with other children for them to follow.
- Four or five pieces of apparatus are placed in the hall and working in pairs, the children are asked to draw an outline plan or map of the hall, marking North. Each child is asked to stand in a space in the hall and to mark it on the map by drawing an X and then drawing a Y to represent where the partner is standing. They are then asked to draw a dotted line on the map to join X and Y. Each child in the pair then walks the route drawn on the map.

Introducing setting the map to North, coordinates and map reading

These activities require a grid map of the hall or outdoor area (with North marked on the map and in the hall or outdoor area), some coloured spots and grid references. Coloured spots are stuck around the hall/area. The children are divided into groups and each group is supplied with a grid map and a set of grid references. At each grid reference in the hall/area, there is a coloured spot. The children have to find the coloured spots and stick them onto their map at the appropriate reference.

Woodland trail and scavenger hunt   The children follow a trail of arrows, streamers, stones, markers, etc. within a specific area. At each marker there could be a task to carry out. The children could also be asked to find specific items within a certain area. A basic map with distinguishing features could be used.

'Star' orienteering   Between 15 and 20 maps of the school grounds with particular points (control points) marked on each are needed. Each control point on the map has a number and a letter. Cards with each number and letter are placed at each of the control points represented on the maps. Plain cards are also needed for the children to write on.

Working in pairs, the children are each given a map with a start point and a control point marked on it. From the starting point they must orientate their map and run to the control point marked on their map, collect a letter and number, which they write down on a card. They then return to the start and exchange their map for another and set off to find a new control point. This continues until all the control points have been visited. Each number represents the position of a control point. The letters when collected are an anagram of a particular word and must be rearranged to solve the anagram.

The advantage of this activity is that the children always return to base so it is easy to monitor the class. As with any lesson the children should come together at the end to share and discuss what they have experienced, what they feel they have achieved and where they might progress from this point. Each child should be encouraged to look positively at their achievements, for example, being able to listen to others and take on board their ideas, understanding the points of the compass and being able to use it. The teacher should recognize these achievements and ensure that they are consolidated and developed further in subsequent lessons.

ATHLETIC ACTIVITIES

The QCA document *Maintaining breadth and balance* (1998) states that in athletic activities, by the end of Key Stage 2 most children are able to 'compare and improve their performance and techniques in running, jumping and throwing'.

Athletics develops the individual skills of throwing, running and jumping as well as maintaining and developing muscular strength and endurance, flexibility and cardiovascular fitness. Skills related to timing, measuring and recording will also be developed where children are given these responsibilities.

Lesson Planning, Teaching Points and Organization for Athletic Activities

A group teaching strategy is preferable as this can foster greater activity levels and safety. Teachers should include whole-class introductory warm-up activities and concluding activities, together with a number of activities to develop techniques in the areas of running, throwing and jumping around which groups of children move. Clearly, this sort of 'circus' teaching strategy gives some degree of responsibility to the children themselves and rules and routines to maximize safe practice should be taught and implemented before using a 'rotating group' style of management.

Teachers should be clear about their learning objectives, but these may extend over a number of lessons as each group experiences the various activities available.

Teaching Points

Teachers will need to learn the techniques that are appropriate for primary age children so that suitable teaching points can be given to enhance performance and ensure progression. For example:

- Running – using the arms thrusting in the opposite direction to increase speed.
- Throwing – making sure that the opposite leg to the throwing arm is forward and that the body weight 'follows through' during the throw.
- Jumping – encouraging the use of the arms to help increase the distance of the jump.

By carefully observing the children, the range of movement responses will be seen and it will be possible to be able to teach from observation.

Organization

Equipment, working areas and recording sheets (perhaps on clipboards) and pens or pencils must all be ready before the lesson. The children should be taught to take some responsibility for management, setting up and clearing away equipment. It is important to include opportunities for the children to measure and time their results and time should be allowed for recording the results back in the classroom. The data collected could be used for maths or science lessons.

Task or activity cards made by the teacher and/or children can be a useful resource, particularly if they show or explain teaching points.

Safety

Safety is always an important consideration in physical education and especially in athletic activities. Few primary schools will have specialist facilities such as long jump pits, so will need to tailor their planning and teaching to suit their resources. Long jumps from a standing position do not need pits and are an excellent activity for primary children to experience, but not for a whole lesson. Athletic activities, by their very nature tend to be 'explosive' and can put great strain and pressure on specific areas of the body if repeated for any length of time. Without specialist facilities, high jump is best left until Key Stage 3.

The following safety tips should be considered when planning and teaching athletic activities.

■ The type of activities each group will experience in any one lesson should be planned with care. For instance, jumping for length and then moving on to throwing for distance does not put pressure on the same body parts.
■ Sufficient space must be allowed for and between activities.
■ The positioning of activities must be thought out carefully at the planning stage, for example, the direction of throwing activities.
■ It is very important that the children remain well behind the throwing line and that all objects thrown are retrieved at the same time.
■ Landing areas, when teaching standing jumping for length, should be non-slip surfaces, such as mats or dry grass, sand or a sprung floor. Children should not jump for length onto hard concrete surfaces or slippery surfaces such as wet grass.
■ Warm-up activities should be included in the lesson planning and also opportunities for the development of techniques and refinement of skills.
■ It is advisable to use adapted equipment when necessary, e.g. shuttlecocks for throwing in restricted areas.

Measurement and Timing

Each group of children should take some responsibility for measuring and timing their own work using tape measures and stop watches as necessary. It is advisable to spend some time in the classroom giving information about how to use them effectively. Each child should be encouraged to take turns at measuring and timing.

Chalk marks, Unifix cubes or even 'lollipop sticks' can aid recording distance when repeated attempts, for example at long jump, are being made. The cubes or lollipop sticks can be moved to mark the best effort and then the actual distance measured at the end of the activity.

'Take your marks, set, go!' is a simple and effective starting signal. The children can be shown how to use their finger joints, rather than the pad of their finger to press a stop watch. A simple recording system can be devised for each child or the children could be encouraged to devise their own systems.

Sports Days

Many schools are moving away from the 'traditional' sports day where a few children are active and everyone else spectates. A format where maximum participation is encouraged through the children being placed in mixed age groups and rotating round a 'circus' of throwing, running and jumping activities is becoming more popular. Points can still be awarded and the winning teams acknowledged.

Awards Schemes

There are a variety of published schemes that can aid lesson planning and can be an incentive to the children. The Amateur Athletic Association is a useful source of information.

Chapter 3

Physical Education and Other Areas of the Whole Curriculum

Physical Education and the Use of Language

Physical activity is a very effective vehicle for learning language as the language is linked to action. Toddlers and young children often keep up a running commentary on what they are doing. The daughter of one of the authors (named Rachel) would continually talk to herself between the ages of 18 months and 4 years. She would say, 'Careful Eel! (she couldn't quite manage Rachel in the early days) Don't fall down', 'Jump off the sofa', 'Climbing. One hand, two hands. One hand, two hands.'

Translating movement into spoken language in a variety of contexts offers a treasure chest of descriptive, directional and action words for children to explore and experience. When children reach school, it is important that these links between movement and language are encouraged and not denied.

There is no need for children to work silently during their physical education lessons. In the early years, children will want to keep up their own commentary on what they are doing. They will need to communicate in order to move apparatus together in gymnastics, roll a ball to each other in games or follow a partner in dance. In all the six areas of activity children should be encouraged to make constructive comments on both their own and the performance of others to improve the accuracy, quality and variety of their performance. Learning to cooperate, compete, solve problems and make decisions are all part of what physical education is about in the primary school. Without language most of these aspects would be impossible.

In physical education children will experience the infinite number of ways in which verbs like throw, kick, balance, roll, spin, etc. can be interpreted. They will also experience adverbs that describe the quality of the verb, e.g. 'Kick powerfully', 'Skip lightly', 'Roll smoothly', 'Dance jerkily', etc.

Teacher talk is the usual method of task setting in physical education and is

TABLE 3.1 Physical education and links with other curriculum areas

	Mathematics	Science/Technology
Gymnastics	Language of comparatives, e.g. next to, before, bigger than, taller than Recognizing patterns, e.g. travel, jump, land, travel, etc Describing and discussing shapes and patterns Body shape Symmetry/Asymmetry Understanding angles, quarter turns, half turns, right angles, rotation Estimating distance Language of number in practical ways Patterns on floor	Recognizing hazards and risk Planning safe movements Naming parts of the body Recognizing similarities and differences between themselves and others Forces – body weight Observation and description of movements Selection of equipment Awareness of surfaces for different tasks
Dance	Symmetry/Asymmetry Floor patterns and pathways, e.g. square, circle Body shape Understanding angles, quarter turns, half-turns, right angles, rotation Vocabulary: curved, straight, angled, etc. Remembering number sequences Rhythms	Naming parts of the body Recognizing similarities and differences between themselves and others Exploring aspects of science in dance, e.g. push/pull, electrical circuits, materials, growth Creating own music and recording Making costumes, masks, props to support or stimulate dance ideas
Games and Athletics	Games and athletic activities can offer purposeful, real-life contexts for estimating, measuring, recording and then data handling Working out angles, etc. Probability	Forces and motion – sending and receiving of objects, trajectories of throws, hits, kicks, etc. Effects of friction, slowing moving objects Selection of most appropriate equipment, e.g. best types of bat for hitting Strategies and tactics in games – discussing options Making informed choices about distance, force
Health-related Fitness, Outdoor Education and Swimming	Problem solving Using coordinates, e.g. map references Directions – NSEW Orienteering – points of compass Cooperative bench games using maths as basis Observation of maths in swimming, e.g. symmetrical/asymmetrical strokes	Learning about the effects of exercise on the body, blood flow, pulse rate, respiration Recognizing hazards and risk Naming parts of the body Recognizing similarities and differences between themselves and others Floating and sinking Forces and motion – in swimming, pushes and pulls through the water

Language/Drama	Humanities	Music/Art
Observing and describing movements Making judgements about the work of others Giving feedback to a partner Words for actions, space, body shape, direction, speed, etc. Directional, positional language – on, off, side by side Reinforcement of colours – red group, blue stool, etc.	Physical activities in different cultures and times, e.g. Japanese links with healthy body and mind, Victorian ladies seen as fragile History of gymnastics – Romans	Awareness of aesthetics in movements Visual awareness of shape and form Language to express awareness Simple 'aerobic'-type activities to music as part of warm-up in physical education
Responding to stories, poems, nursery rhymes Descriptive words for movements, e.g. slithering, gliding, etc. Expressing feelings and moods – ideas for own writing Collaboration for creating group story, poem in movement – sense of story Production of dances for others to see	Responding to music Developing sense of rhythm and pulse Dance and music from different cultures Dance and music from different ages Dance in human spiritual responses Making costumes, masks, props to support or stimulate dance ideas Creating own music and recording	
Observing and describing movements Making judgements about the work of others Giving feedback to a partner Words for action/space, direction/speed, etc. Directional, positional language – on, off, side by side Reinforcement of colours – red marker, blue ball, etc.	Games as a topic: Olympic Games, games in different societies, currently and in past Games in different cultures Games and equality issues	Writing own team song, jingle Designing own 'strip', flags, badges, etc.
Awareness of others Working as a team Identifying own feelings Showing sensitivity to others Reaching consensus Writing about feelings and experiences, e.g. water, swimming	Recognizing where things are Expressing views about the environment	Swimming whilst singing a song, to help develop rhythm of stroke Simple 'aerobic'-type activities to music as part of warm-up in physical education

another way of developing children's language. The names of particular body parts such as hands, wrists, elbows and joints can be learned as can the technical names for new equipment such as movement table, plank, quoit, and hoop. Children soon realize that the same name can be used for different objects: in gymnastics a box is not the thing that new shoes come in and a bench is not something you sit on in the park!

In setting tasks in physical education teachers use a great deal of directional, spatial and temporal language, e.g. 'Run forwards using large steps', 'Throw your beanbag to land inside the hoop', 'Slide smoothly down the bench on your back or front'. In order to respond appropriately in movement, children need to interpret these quite complex instructions. Teachers need to ensure that the instructions they give are clear, specific and concise and often supported by example or demonstration in order to develop children's listening skills and extend their understanding.

During the later stages of the primary school, children's descriptions and judgements of their work and that of others, the feedback they give to others, the questions they ask and their own planning and evaluations of their actions are all opportunities for developing speaking and listening skills.

In dance particularly, language has an important role in helping children to develop ways of moving that express mood, feelings and ideas. The 'Descriptive words for dance actions' in Figure 2.7, p. 51, are useful stimuli.

The rich potential of physical education for developing children's understanding and use of language should be exploited. We have all heard some version of the saying, 'Show me and I see, tell me and I hear but let me do, and I'll understand'. Never has this been so true as with physical education and language.

Cross-curricular Matters

Physical education can make significant contributions to the development of cross-curriculum skills, not least through its use of problem-solving methods and approaches across the six areas of activity. The adoption of 'games for understanding' is an example of the way in which activities traditionally associated with highly didactic methods can be approached through a problem-solving perspective. The immediacy of the effects of problem solving on the active involvement of children in the process, safety and performance reinforce the effectiveness of physical education in providing children with the opportunities to acquire and apply skills in a variety of situations.

Physical education can also support children's knowledge, skills and understanding across the whole curriculum. The chart in Table 3.1 identifies some of the areas that link effectively with physical education.

Health Education

Whilst health education is not considered to be a curriculum subject in its own right, a number of National Curriculum subjects are expected to contribute to children's knowledge and understanding of the very wide area of health. A good physical education curriculum can have a significant influence on long-term health, attitudes and behaviour. It can:

- develop a positive attitude to physical activity and health
- make children aware of the changes that occur to their bodies during physical education lessons
- motivate pupils to participate in a range of physical activities, thus aiding development of cardiovascular health, flexibility, muscular strength and endurance
- encourage good posture and the appropriate use of the body
- teach pupils to warm up before exercise and recover from exercise
- assist in the management of existing conditions e.g. asthma
- promote mental well-being, good mood and positive self-image
- provide knowledge required for safe participation in and effective planning of individually appropriate exercise programmes.

The QCA document *Maintaining Breadth and Balance* describes physical education at Key Stage 1 as being partly about children becoming: 'aware of the changes that occur to their bodies as they exercise and recognize the short term effects'. By Key Stage 2 this has progressed to: 'They sustain energetic activity over appropriate periods of time and understand the short-term effects of exercise' (QCA 1998).

The key aspects drawn from the programmes of study for Key Stage 1 and Key Stage 2 also relate to aspects of health education. At Key Stage 1: 'Developing a positive attitude to physical activity and health' and 'Learning safe practices … learning how to lift, carry and place equipment safely' (QCA 1998) are important. However, at Key Stage 2 this has progressed to: 'Developing positive attitudes to physical activity and healthy lifestyles' and 'Learning safe practices. In particular, following rules, laws, codes and safety procedures for different activities and knowing how to warm up and recover from exercise' (QCA 1998).

Although the QCA document focuses on positive attitudes to physical exercise, the effects of exercise and safe practice, teaching and learning in physical education can contribute in a much wider way. For instance, in swimming, water safety will be discussed and through the school policy for physical education clothing, hygiene and puberty are likely to be discussed.

All the areas of health education 'within the skipping rope' might be addressed through the vehicle of physical education and the list is certainly not exhaustive (see Figure 3.1).

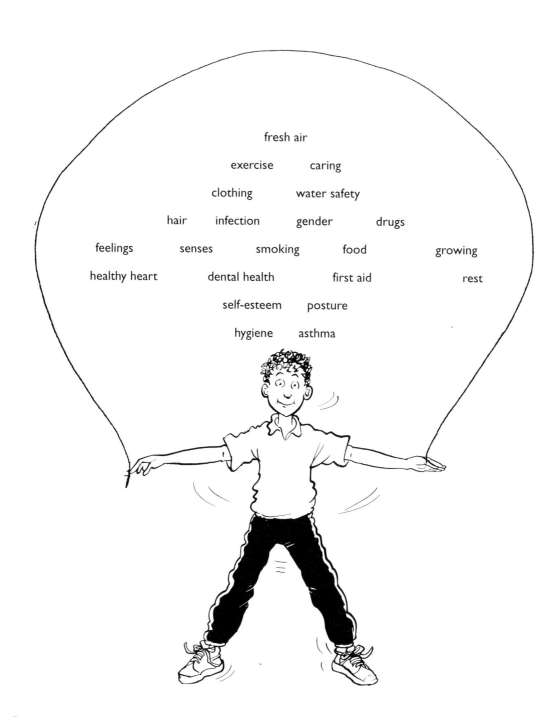

FIGURE 3.1 Areas of health education within the 'skipping rope'

Strategies for Including Aspects of Health-related Fitness and Exercise in Primary Physical Education Teaching

The health-related aspects of the QCA document, together with the other contributions that physical education can make to children's knowledge and understanding of health education should be taught alongside the six areas of activity. They should permeate physical education teaching and not be discrete areas of their own. There are many strategies that teachers can use to help children develop their health education knowledge and understanding through physical education.

Questioning

Questioning can be useful to draw attention to the effects of exercise on the children's (and your!) bodies during any type of physical education lesson. For example:

- You might ask, 'I wonder why your faces look very red?'
- You could ask the children to find their pulse. The carotid pulse in the neck can be the easiest to find.
- You could ask them if they know why their pulse is faster after physical activity than before and whether they can record in various ways the increase and gradual decrease in pulse rate after activity.
- You could ask the children to feel their heartbeat by placing the right hand on their chest. Ask them to show the beating speed by moving the left hand in time with the pulse.
- You could ask them why is the heart beating faster after exercise and link this with what they might have learned in the science curriculum.
- You could ask them why they are perspiring after exercise.

Appropriate use of open-ended questioning, rather than didactic instruction, can be useful to develop understanding of safety issues.
  You could also:

- ask why a physical education 'kit' is necessary
- discuss the arrangement of gymnastic apparatus with the class, perhaps in the classroom first of all
- discuss lifting techniques (straight backs, bent knees, etc.)
- ask the children to come to some agreement (with your guidance) about appropriate rules for carrying equipment.

Fitness

Levels of fitness as demonstrated by cardiovascular health, flexibility and muscular strength will vary a great deal amongst the children. Those who consider themselves to be less skilful in physical education may well be very flexible and if this is emphasized by the teacher, it can be effective in boosting the self-esteem of these children. Be careful that you do not always emphasize muscular strength and cardiovascular health.

Lesson Planning

Lessons should be planned with appropriate warm-up and concluding activities. You need to consider:

- the space available
- which body parts will be mainly used during the rest of the lesson. Ensure that these particularly are warmed up
- how active the rest of the lesson will be
- keeping organizational aspects to a minimum
- what equipment is easily available
- the weather (!)

Lessons should be planned to allow for maximum activity, keeping waiting or 'standing around' time to a minimum. You might:

- consider organizing the class in pre-arranged groups to aid management
- establish a system for collection/setting up of equipment that can last for a number of weeks
- use a small group/individual to demonstrate an activity rather than needing to explain it verbally to the whole class. A demonstration can be worth a thousand words and can take much less time.

Lessons should be planned with an overall balance in mind. You might:

- need to ensure that the warm-up part of the lesson is very active if the rest of the lesson is less so
- need to consider including some of all three aspects of fitness (cardiovascular, flexibility and muscular strength) in your lesson.

Personal and Social Education

Physical education has an important role to play in developing children's personal skills; 'Citizenship' is currently being promoted as an area on which schools are being asked to focus. Spiritual, moral, social and cultural development can all be promoted and observed through physical education.

Through physical education children develop such skills and qualities as:

- good sporting behaviour as a participant team member and spectator
- an ability to work cooperatively with others by being a member of a team or group
- the ability to cope with success and limitations in performance
- sensitivity towards individual differences by adapting responses to others' levels of skill
- a spirit of adventure with appropriate risk assessment
- self-discipline
- self-reliance
- a sense of responsibility by planning and undertaking safe health-related exercise
- being mindful of others and the environment.

Physical education is not solely about being active, but children's experiences whilst they are active can have a lasting effect. In physical education they are not merely bystanders or passive recipients of advice or instructions but are actively involved in what is happening; they are making their own decisions and solving their own problems.

Chapter 4

Planning for Physical Education at Key Stages 1 and 2

In order for class teachers to plan and teach appropriate series of physical education lessons which maintain pace, motivation and challenge for pupils, medium- and long-term planning and school policies need to be in place.

The School Physical Education Policy

What Might Be Included?

A: Philosophy

Aims of school
Policy statement
School's physical education aims

B: Curriculum

Schemes of work for each key stage and/or year group
Timetable organization for year groups
Assessment, recording and reporting – processes explained
Poor weather policy

C: Children

Assessment, recording and reporting strategies

Special needs provision
Teaching and learning styles and strategies
Policy on grouping children

D: Staffing

Teaching and non-teaching staff responsibilities, qualifications and duties
Staff development needs
Procedures for supporting new teachers and trainee teachers

E: Pupil procedures

Beginning and ending of lessons
Medical conditions and records
Clothing and jewellery

F: Safety

Guidelines and risk assessment
Emergencies – First aid equipment and qualified personnel

G: Resources

Plans of hall, gymnasium, field, playground, etc.
Equipment/resources inventory and how/where stored
Maintenance schedules
Capitation/spending audits
Staff reference materials – books, videos, cassette tapes
Physical education books for pupils

H: Community

Use of community facilities
Use of expertise within the community
Use of school's facilities by community
Links with partnership schools
Telephone numbers and addresses of outside agencies, clubs, societies and
    other useful contacts
Procedures for fixtures/sports/activity days

I: Continuing professional development

Current teachers
Newly qualified teachers
Teachers who are new to the school
Learning support assistants
Play leaders, extra-curricular helpers

J: Extra-curricular activities

Rational/Aims and objectives
Teams/clubs
Visits
Residential experience
Community help
Major school events

Long-term Planning

In order to ensure a balanced approach to the arrangements for teaching physical education, schools need to establish the total time available for physical education at each key stage and indeed in each year (see Table 4.1).

When the total number of hours per year for physical education is known, the school has to allocate hours to areas of activity, i.e. dance, games and gymnastics for Key Stage 1 and all the above, plus swimming at Key Stage 2 and if possible athletics, outdoor and adventurous activities.

Schools must also decide what proportion of time will be spent on each area. For instance, will games have twice as much time as dance? Will games and gymnastics have the same amounts of time? The 'weighting' given to each area of activity is left for schools to decide.

TABLE 4.1   Example of a long-term plan

	No. of weeks	Hours per week	Total hours
Autumn Term			
Spring Term			
Summer Term			

The example in Table 4.2 shows one school's plan for implementation of the six areas of activity for physical education at Key Stage 2. As you can see, this school allocates three physical education lessons per week throughout the key stage. Your school might have two lessons per week or two per week for half the year and three per week for the rest of the year.

TABLE 4.2 Physical education: whole curriculum planning at Key Stage 2 (example)

Year	Term	No. of weeks	Lesson 1	Lesson 2	Lesson 3
Year 3	Autumn	1st (7)/2nd (8)	O & A/Games	Dance/Dance	Gym/Gym
	Spring	1st (7)/2nd (6)	Games/Games	Dance/Dance	Gym/Gym
	Summer	1st (6)/2nd (6)	Games/Games	Athletics/Athletics	Swimming/Swimming
Year 4	Autumn	1st (7)/2nd (8)	O & A/Games	Dance/Dance	Swimming/Gym
	Spring	1st (7)/2nd (6)	Games/Games	Dance/Dance	Gym/Gym
	Summer	1st (6)/2nd (6)	Games/Games	Athletics/Athletics	Swimming/Swimming
Year 5	Autumn	1st (7)/2nd (8)	Games/Games	Swimming/Swimming	Gym/Gym
	Spring	1st (7)/2nd (6)	Games/Games	Dance/Dance	Gym/Gym
	Summer	1st (6)/2nd (6)	Games/Games	Athletics/Athletics	O & A/O & A
Year 6	Autumn	1st (7)/2nd (8)	Games/Games	Dance/Dance	Gym/Gym
	Spring	1st (7)/2nd (6)	Games/Games	Dance/Dance	Gym/Gym
	Summer	1st (6)/2nd (6)	Games/Games	Swimming/Athletics	O & A/O & A

NOTE: O & A is Outdoor Education and Athletics

Schemes of Work

Once time allocations are clarified, schools should develop schemes of work that give a rationale for physical education within the school and outline the themes and topics for each key stage and often each year group. Schemes should be drawn up in accordance with the current statutory requirements of the National Curriculum, taking into account any non-statutory guidance and should provide an overview of the physical education curriculum throughout that school. Schemes of work should ensure that the children receive a broad and balanced physical education curriculum, provide progression and continuity and give a framework from which medium- and short-term plans can be written and implemented.

Medium-term Planning

Once schools have developed schemes of work and established how much time will be available for each area of activity at each key stage, then either the physical education subject leader or each class teacher needs to develop medium-term plans – units of work.

Each unit of work should show the teacher's planning outline for each half-term block of activity. Units of work should indicate:

- intended teaching and learning objectives, which should also be the focus for assessment
- an outline of lesson content, skills to be developed and resources required
- progression from previous work and use of assessment information from previous teaching
- opportunities for children to plan, perform and evaluate their work with emphasis on performance
- support required for children with special educational needs
- assessment foci, opportunities and procedures
- resources required
- time available
- opportunities for consolidation of skills acquired in literacy, numeracy and ICT opportunities to exploit cross-curricular learning with science and other foundation subjects
- opportunities to contribute to children's spiritual, moral, personal, social and cultural development.

Review and Evaluation

Once time allocation, schemes and units of work are in place, there will be a need for continuous review and modification by physical education subject leaders as well as class teachers as a result of the children's responses and progress.

Short-term Planning

At this stage, with time allocation and schemes and units of work in place, teachers can plan their sequence of individual lessons in detail (see Appendix B, p. 164 for a blank lesson-plan format sheet). Individual lesson plans should indicate:

- clear teaching and learning objectives
- an appropriate lesson structure including warm-up, skill development and cool-down activities
- a progressive series of activities closely related to the teaching and learning objectives in which all children in the class can succeed at some level
- opportunities for differentiation
- the key points for demonstrations
- the use of subject-specific vocabulary
- teaching points related to the teaching and learning objective, i.e. teachers need to consider prior to the lesson what is likely to observed in the children's movement responses and what might be said to aid progression. It can be useful to consider the likely 'mistakes' that the children might make, e.g. in an overarm throw, having the same leg forward as the throwing arm or taking weight on the fingertips instead of the whole hand during gymnastics
- opportunities for children to consolidate their progress through practice
- opportunities for children to evaluate their own performance and that of others
- assessment opportunities and foci
- organizational procedures, e.g. (a) how the children will be grouped at various points in the lesson – individuals, pairs, small groups; (b) how equipment will be distributed and collected effectively and safely
- an awareness of potential safety hazards and how these will be minimized
- the resources required and how these will be placed and spaced.

Aspects of Lesson Planning

At Key Stage 1 and Key Stage 2 lessons may vary in length up to a maximum of 60 minutes, according to the age of the pupils. Five-year-olds may only be able to sustain 20 minutes of activity and in cold weather a brisk 10 minutes of games outside may be more appropriate than half an hour inside. Lessons that are longer than 60 minutes, even with older pupils, are often wasted because pupils' levels of concentration may be limited.

Structuring Games Lessons

Warm-up/introductory activity (2–3 minutes)

- The introductory activity should prepare the body for what is to come later in the lesson and should leave the children warm and slightly out of breath.
- It should be purposeful and vigorous and a preparation for what is to come later in the lesson.
- It could involve footwork activities and movement in different ways, e.g. dodging, hopping, jumping, skipping, walking.
- Actions and movements that will be used and developed later in the lesson should be chosen.

Development: individual skills (7–10 minutes)

- A variety of equipment, e.g. bats, bean bags, hoops, ropes, shuttlecocks, skittles and quoits should be used.
- Perhaps specially designed equipment for pupils with physical disabilities could be used.
- The development of individual skills may involve exploration, followed by directed practice skills.

Development: small-group games (15 minutes)

- Individual skills can now be related to small-sided games situations in twos, threes or fours – small-group size = maximum participation.
- Some of the games may be made up and refined by the pupils.

Concluding activities (1–2 minutes)

- These are final activities that bring the class together – often a calming, cooling-down activity.

■ A short discussion about what has been learned (either whilst still in the teaching space or back in the classroom) can be highly beneficial in reinforcing the learning objective.

Structuring Gymnastics Lessons

Warm-up/introductory activity (2–3 minutes)

■ The introductory activity should prepare the body for what is to come later in the lesson and should leave the children warm and slightly out of breath.
■ Some whole-body actions should be included.
■ Some travel around all the available space should also be included.

Development – floor work (7–10 minutes)

■ The theme of the lesson such as travel/weight-bearing activities should be developed through focused but open-ended tasks set by the teacher.
■ Activities should then be linked to produce sequences on the floor.

Development – apparatus (15 minutes)

■ The theme of the lesson is developed on apparatus through focused but open-ended tasks set by the teacher.
■ Activities should be linked to produce sequences on the apparatus.

Concluding activities (1–2 minutes)

■ These are final activities that bring the class together – often a calming, cooling-down activity.
■ A short discussion about what has been learned (either whilst still in the teaching space or back in the classroom) can be highly beneficial in reinforcing the learning objective.

Structuring Dance Lessons

Warm-up/introductory activity (2–3 minutes)

■ This should prepare the body for what is to come later in the lesson and should leave the children warm and slightly out of breath.
■ Activities that encourage individuals to move freely, involving travel and the development of body awareness should be used.

Development (8–10 minutes)

■ This section could also include work on awareness of the body space, actions and dynamics.
■ Main movement ideas selected for the dance should be explored.
■ The main ideas should be developed in a variety of ways using repetition and contrast.

The dance (10–15 minutes)

■ Movements developed earlier should now be linked to create a simple dance performed individually, with a partner or in small groups.
■ Dances should have clear beginnings, middles and ends.

Concluding activities (1–2 minutes)

■ Slow and gentle actions calm the pupils down and provide an orderly finish to the lesson.
■ A short discussion about what has been learned (either whilst still in the teaching space or back in the classroom) can be highly beneficial in reinforcing the learning objective.

Table 4.3 (p. 110) shows an example of how a lesson plan could be set out.

Ensuring That You Actually Teach in Physical Education Lessons

It is possible for teachers to take a whole physical education lesson without actually doing any **teaching**! They will certainly be concentrating on giving instructions and monitoring the children, but may not actually teach.

The cyclical process of task setting, general and specific observation, feedback with teaching points, demonstration, practice and task setting shown below, offers a structure that ensures that some teaching takes place.

■ Set the task – give verbal instructions and use visual demonstration.
■ Watch the class working – get a general overview of the response and understanding.
■ Observe specific children in order to give general encouragement.
■ Observe individuals – give 'public' feedback related to a teaching and learning objective, e.g. 'I can see Jack is really extending his ankles' or 'Gemma is really watching the path of the ball'.
■ Choose a child to demonstrate a teaching point related to a teaching and learning objective.
■ Discuss the demonstration with the children to reinforce the teaching objective.

- Help individual children by giving teaching points and making suggestions.
- Improve the quality of performance – e.g. 'Stretch your fingers when you balance'.
- Look at good performances and discuss why they are good with the children.
- Give enough time for the children to practise the task.
- Set the next task. (See Study Sheet 11.)

Lesson Evaluation and Assessment of Teacher Performance

After a lesson it is important that teachers evaluate their own teaching critically and use this to improve their effectiveness. Teachers need to consider whether the teaching and learning objectives have been achieved, whether organization and management was appropriate, were a range of teaching strategies used and many, many other points that may affect a lesson. It is useful to ask a series of questions to help focus on certain aspects of the lesson in order to evaluate teaching and learning (see Table 4.4).

Lesson Pace and Children's Involvement and Response

Young children are naturally active and in physical education lessons in particular, they have a right to expect to be active. A teacher's lack of enthusiasm and poor planning and organizational skills can easily lead to inactive pupils who often express their frustration through poor behaviour. Most children want to be active and teachers need to work with this desire and not aim to restrict or even squash it altogether (see Figure 4.1).

Differentiation

An important way to encourage children to be involved and responsive is to ensure that they can achieve success in the lesson but also feel challenged by the activities: differentiation is crucial.

Planning and implementing a differentiated physical education curriculum for individual children of different abilities is demanding. Probably the best that might be achieved as a starting point will be making provision for groups of children with similar needs, but it is necessary to aim to:

- build on the past achievement of individual children
- plan specific teaching objectives which develop the skills, knowledge and understanding of all children

TABLE 4.3   An example of a lesson plan for Key Stage 1 or 2

Area of activity: Unit of work:

Teaching and learning objectives: Assessment focus:

Date: Class: Age: No of children:

Lesson structure and timing	Progressive activities
Warm-up	
Development	
Conclusion/Cool-down	

Lesson number:

Duration: Venue: Resources: (Use overleaf for plan
                                                   of apparatus layout)

Differentiation possibilities	Teaching points and feedback	Management and safety

TABLE 4.4   Questions to help and evaluate teaching and learning

Did I ... ?	Did the children ... ?
effectively manage the changing and transfer from classroom to the physical education environment effectively and have the working space and equipment already prepared?	change quickly and sensibly?
explain tasks clearly and concisely?	understand the tasks set?
motivate the children?	attempt the tasks, or do what they most enjoy?
develop the children's understanding of subject specific language?	understand my use of language?
praise positive effort?	all receive positive feedback?
maintain an appropriate working atmosphere?	work purposefully?
use focused demonstration appropriately?	gain anything from observing demonstrations?
allow time to practise a repetition?	improve the quality of their work through practice and repetition?
monitor safety at all times?	work with regard to their own safety and that of others?
show enthusiasm?	show enthusiasm?
encourage the children by my tone of voice, posture and gesture?	gain in confidence?
wear appropriate clothing/footwear?	enjoy the lesson and feel successful?

Then ask yourself:

To what degree did I achieve my teaching and learning objectives?

Were the teaching points given focused on the teaching and learning objectives?

What was the balance of activity against watching, listening etc.?

How could the aim for 'maximum activity for the maximum amount of time' be improved?

Were the tasks appropriate for the particular group of children?

Did I modify the tasks for different skill levels?

Did the quality of the children's movements improve?

Were the children encouraged to be creative/imaginative during the lesson?

And lastly, ... if I were to repeat this lesson in the future what would I change/modify? (See Study Sheets 12 and 13.)

Clarity of purpose and direction
Appropriate pace and timing
High activity levels
Children involved both physically and mentally

lead to active children and reduced control/discipline difficulties and

High work rate
On task
Good concentration
Reduced teacher talk
Enjoyment

Unstructured lessons
Lack of activity
Lack of involvement
Boredom

lead to inactive children and increased control/discipline difficulties and

Mental participation reduced
Physical participation reduced
Increased teacher talk
Low work rate
Off task

FIGURE 4.1   Which scenario is the 'best fit' for your physical education teaching?

■ be creative about removing barriers to participation particularly where these apply to children with special needs
■ provide opportunities for all children to experience success and enjoyment regardless of their levels of ability.

Planning for Differentiation

Planning for differentiation should cover:

■ how to group children – ability/mixed ability, pairs/groups, friendship groups or individuals
■ setting a range of related but different tasks according to ability and experience (differentiation by task) or by setting open-ended tasks that can be interpreted and successfully achieved at many levels (differentiation by outcome)

- resources – variety of equipment and apparatus for different levels of ability/experience
- pupil activity – variety of tasks, different pupil roles and responsibilities, different allocations of time and variations of pace within the lesson to meet the needs of different levels of ability
- other opportunities – extra-curricular activities, introducing children to local clubs, the development of excellence and interest groups.

Individual and Small-group Work

In order to achieve a range of work suitable for differing abilities and stages of development within a class and to maximize on participation, space and equipment available, small-group work is an essential component of most physical education lessons. However the organization and management of group work can cause difficulties for teachers, particularly for those who are inexperienced, but this should not be a reason to resort to whole-class teaching as the only means of organizing children in physical education.

Teachers, particularly new teachers, need to revise and develop their teaching styles and strategies continually in order to implement a differentiated curriculum that maximizes participation. Some parts of the lesson will be directed by the teacher with the whole class following the same task at the same time, but in a well-balanced lesson there will be times when the children are engaged in small-group work that is more appropriate to their individual needs.

Individual and group work can be both advantageous and challenging for both the children and their teacher.

Individual and small group work can offer advantages to teachers and children

- Work can be presented in ways that are most appropriate to meet the needs of individuals and groups of children.
- Children achieve a greater level of participation and involvement and hence, motivation.
- Children can begin to take more responsibility for learning, organization and safety.
- Children have opportunities to develop skills of observation, planning and evaluation as well as skills that promote citizenship, such as responsibility and leadership.
- Children's social and moral values can be developed by sharing the responsibility for their responses to tasks set, the behaviour within the groups and the quality of work.

Individual and small-group work can offer challenges to teachers

Teachers need to consider how to:

- group the children. Mixed ability, mixed gender, friendship groups, other ways
- minimize time spent organizing the children into groups
- minimize time spent setting tasks/organizing equipment for a number of groups
- observe a number of groups and be able to give appropriate feedback/teaching points
- maintain an appropriate noise level
- be able to see all the children at all times and ensure that they can always see the teacher
- ensure maximum safety levels when a number of different activities are happening at once
- achieve immediate attention, silence and stillness from the class when required
- plan work specifically for groups or individuals rather than for vague whole-class needs.

Individual and small-group work can offer challenges to children

Children need to learn how to:

- form relationships within the group
- work with children who do or do not want to work together
- cope with decision making within the group
- feel valued and observed if the teacher is focusing on other groups
- concentrate and 'stay on task' when the teacher is not with them
- ask for the teacher's help or support.

Differentiation by Task and/or Outcome

In physical education, the two most important methods of differentiation are by task and by outcome.

By task ...

This is achieved when pupils who are pursuing the same area of activity are given a range of different but related tasks according to ability and experience.

Pupils might work through a range of increasingly challenging tasks according to their level of attainment. For example, in games, aiming or shooting-type tasks might be differentiated in the following ways:

■ using balls of differing sizes and /or weights
■ varying the height and /or distance from the goal or target.

In an 'over-the-net-type' of activity, the task might be differentiated by:

■ varying the size of the court
■ allowing numerous/few/no bounces
■ allowing children to self-feed or bounce feed
■ using a variety of types of ball, e.g. slower, low-bounce, or large, soft balls.

In an invasion-type game, the task might be differentiated by:

■ having an unequal numbers of players on each side e.g. three versus one, three versus two, four versus two
■ adapting rules so that every team member must play the ball before a goal can be scored
■ varying pitch size, goal size, type and size of ball.

In matching activities to the abilities of the children, teachers may need to develop a series of developmental tasks. For example, a Key Stage 1 child may need assistance with sending and receiving a ball, so a large ball might be used in a rolling motion in order to send and receive with success. If this proves to be too difficult, then a bean bag might be used in a sliding motion.

In paired or small-group games activities, teachers also need to encourage children to decide what should be their own optimum distance from each other. For instance, standing too close together when sending and receiving gives little time for the receiver to make appropriate judgements and act accordingly, but being too far apart might lead to inaccuracy by the sender.

By outcome ...

This involves setting tasks that are appropriate for children's starting levels and allow progress to be made by all the class or group. The children use their knowledge and understanding to achieve success at different levels. For instance, children might find different ways of passing a ball to outwit an opponent in games or to move along a bench in gymnastics. Some children might use advanced methods unachievable by others in the class or group.

Progression

Without progression, children underachieve. Whilst the 'Expectations' section in the QCA document *Maintaining Breadth and Balance* (1998) provides a framework for achievement expected at the end of each key stage, in physical education, making individual activities progressive is one of the biggest challenges facing primary teachers. Ensuring that children progress to reach their potential requires teachers to consider activities in terms of difficulty and quality and to give children opportunities to plan and evaluate their own performance.

Planning involves children being able to:

think ahead
imagine the finished action
anticipate responses from others
compose movements
devise appropriate tactics
select appropriate movements/responses.

Performing involves children being able to:

make appropriate movements/responses
link movements together
be competent and versatile
practise and refine skills.

Evaluating involves children being able to:

observe in a focused manner
compare with accuracy
describe using increasingly technical language
make judgements about their own performance and that of others
use movement experiences and understanding in future planning and
    performing.

Whilst progression is important in each of these three strands, the emphasis should be on performing.

In physical education there are two main elements of progression – difficulty and quality. The following shows an example of the way in which an activity can be analysed in terms of difficulty and quality in each of the three strands (planning, performing and evaluating).

Analysing Difficulty and Quality in a Key Stage 2 Games Activity

Two versus one practice: A large ball is passed with the hands below head height to a partner. The third person attempts to intercept or touch the ball. The emphasis in this practice is on the roles of the two players in possession of the ball (see Table 4.5).

TABLE 4.5   Analysing difficulty and quality in a two versus one games activity

	Difficulty	*Quality*
Planning	Plan which type of pass to use to easily defeat the third person, i.e. bounce, chest, shoulder or head-height pass. Decide how to use feints and dodges to outwit the third person	Make an action plan of how to be successful. Decide how to properly execute the pass to prevent the person in the middle from touching or intercepting the ball
Performing	Implement the plan and adapt if necessary. Use a range of types of pass and pass quickly	Make each pass with ease, control and at a good height for catching. Ensure that the partner can catch the ball without moving too far
Evaluating	Consider the number of different types of pass used and how quickly they were made. Was the third person made to chase around without too much success?	Consider the success of the activity by the number of successful passes. Were the passes easy to catch, accurate and at a good speed? Consider whether the techniques used in making the various passes were acceptable

In what ways can 'difficulty' be used to differentiate tasks?

Performance may be made more difficult or challenging by requiring:

- the development of a greater variety of movements within a task, e.g. variety of speed, direction, use of various body parts
- pupils to find different ways of performing a task, e.g. in passing a ball to a partner
- the transfer of travelling and manipulative skills from one area of activity to another, e.g. travelling and jumping in gymnastic activities could help improve performance in athletic activities and dance
- improved balance, e.g. in some gymnastic activities, dance and in outdoor and adventurous activities
- greater strength, e.g. in increasing personal performance in athletic activities or swimming

- improved coordination, e.g. in combining activities in dance and gymnastic activities
- less time in performing effectively in activities requiring quick decision-making, such as matching or mirroring a partner's actions
- less space, e.g. game skills are more challenging when working in a restricted area
- fewer options, e.g. in the number of ways of passing a ball in an invasion game or smaller targets at which to aim a ball
- development from single to multiple actions, e.g. combining a run, a jump and a roll into a controlled sequence
- development from concrete to abstract ideas, e.g. expressing moods, feelings and ideas in movement after developing the basic actions of travelling, jumping, turning, gesture and stillness
- development from simple to complex knowledge of the activity, e.g. being taught more advanced techniques in long jumping, and knowing how to analyse and improve performance.

An example of progression in difficulty of a gymnastic balance

The balance could be made more difficult by the following:

KS1	KS2	KS3
Slightly reducing the base of support	Considering the transition into and out of the balance	Performing the balance with another person

In Which Ways Can 'Quality' Be Used to Improve Performance?

Making progress in the quality of a performance is closely related to physical development and maturation, but can also be identified through tasks requiring:

- better control
- improved form and body tension in gymnastic and dance performances
- better hand and eye coordination in striking activities
- increasing control of the body in developing an effective and efficient swimming stroke.

In order to help children achieve quality in physical education lessons teachers should:

- allow time for repetition, experimentation and refinement
- observe pupils' work and provide positive feedback

- encourage pupil observation of each other's work
- isolate parts of a movement and/or a sequence
- challenge all levels of ability whilst permitting a range of responses
- analyse movement qualities with the children
- progress through material logically, with success for each child at each stage.

Two other elements are important when considering progression: independence and interaction. These relate more to pupils' personal and social development than to skill development.

Independence

Children's independence will develop through:

- taking more initiative and responsibility in planning and evaluating tasks
- becoming more experienced in managing all types of equipment/apparatus
- taking more responsibility for their own actions
- becoming more aware of their own safety and the safety of others
- making increasing use of partnership between the school and the community.

Interaction

Children's communication skills will develop through:

- giving feedback on their own performances and those of others
- developing the ability to cope with success and limitation in performance
- sharing space and resources
- working cooperatively in pairs and in groups
- working competitively against others
- deciding their own groupings.

Chapter 5

Teaching and Management of Physical
Education at Key Stages 1 and 2

Physical education lessons can give inexperienced teachers at least a few
sleepless nights! The teaching space, be it the school hall, playground or field
can make teachers feel vulnerable and open to scrutiny. The children may feel
that the expectations their teacher has of them in the classroom do not apply in
a different environment. The children are not seated at desks but move freely,
sometimes at speed in the space, and safety of course, is a great concern.
Inexperienced teachers are right to be anxious but with attention to
organizational and management matters, good observational skills, careful
planning and an awareness of safety issues and risk assessment, then the
sleepless nights can be kept to a minimum.

Organization and Management (see Figure 5.1)

Organization and management are closely linked. Poorly prepared lessons
usually lead to difficulties in managing and motivating the children. However,
children are usually very anxious to please their teacher. Observation, praise,
sensitivity and constructive feedback as well as subject knowledge are vital to
success for the children and for you. Your aim should be to create a quiet, well-
organized and safe environment that is conducive to learning. There is no
simple recipe for this, as it comes from a mixture of ingredients.

Changing routines and movement to and from the lesson, particularly in the
early years, are as important a part of the children's learning as the lesson
content itself. The mood for the lesson is often 'set' as the children change and
move to the hall, playground or field. If the children are silly, noisy or
boisterous at this stage it would be foolish to begin without establishing control
over the group. This may mean taking them back to the changing area all over

Organization is closely linked to effective control

Remember to think ahead

Gain attention of group – use clear stopping and starting signals

A good demonstration is better than a long explanation

Never give too many instructions at once

Initiate a well-disciplined working environment

Silence whilst working is not required – a buzz of noise is acceptable

Always ensure that equipment/apparatus is handled correctly

Tone of voice is important

It is necessary to make sure you have equipment readily available before the lesson

Observe the activities, offer teaching points and ensure safety

Never leave a large group of children unattended

FIGURE 5.1   Some key points to ensure effective organization and management

again! When working with a new class it is important to set expectations clearly and keep to them.

Try to learn as many of the children's names as soon as possible and use them during the lesson. This is a great asset in being able to manage and motivate the group.

You should only give instructions when you have got the attention of the whole group. It is worth waiting for that moment of complete stillness rather than trying to speak above noise or activity, otherwise many children may not hear what you have to say and also you may lose some of your authority. Consider where you position yourself in relation to the children when you want to speak to them all. Perhaps ask them to group together in front of you. Keeping instructions concise and clear will prevent children having to listen for too long and becoming bored and fidgety. Remember that a demonstration or 'walk through' with a few children may save a great deal of explanation. There is also a limit as to how much the children will actually remember from a long list of instructions and you will need to judge this against the age and experience of the class.

Establish clear 'starting' and 'stopping' signals from the beginning – try to give the impression that you have confidence in your ability to control and motivate the group even if in the early stages you are quaking at the knees! A clap, a word and a 'large gesture' work well. Expect the children to respond quickly to your instructions. Use your eyes to scan the work space. Praise by name those who respond quickly. Getting 'louder' in your delivery the second and third time of asking does not necessarily mean that the children automatically listen any more carefully.

Whilst the children are active, your teaching position needs to be such that you are able to keep all the children within your peripheral field of vision. As you move around the teaching space interacting with the children, keep to the edges rather than the middle as this would mean turning your back on some children. Children need to see you and to know that you can see them.

When setting up work give instructions first, then let some groups of children collect and set up their equipment. When all groups are ready you should check placing and spacing, and let groups all begin working at the same time.

Observation

In physical education you need to use your observational skills for a range of purposes. You need to be able to scan the whole class to check for task compliance, discipline and safety but you also need to be able to focus on individuals in order to make judgements about appropriate feedback/teaching points, the need for differentiation and to make assessments. Teachers need to be skilled observers in order to:

- maintain a safe working environment
- scan for compliance, behaviour and understanding of the tasks set
- be able to give appropriate teaching points to the whole class, groups and individuals
- learn more about child development
- conduct an ongoing check on a child's progress
- make an assessment of a child's abilities, including strengths and areas for development
- make individual plans based on observed needs
- consider strategies for solving problems experienced by a child
- gather information for a child's profile.

With clear teaching and learning objectives, specific assessment foci, established rules and routines which maximize safety, teachers can give themselves the opportunity to observe and assess children during physical education lessons. Inexperienced teachers should aim to focus mainly on one or two children initially until they gain in confidence. With practice and a clear focus, it is surprising how quickly teachers can become able to make judgements about a wide range of children based on the evidence seen during a single lesson.

Presentation of Self

The example you set the children with regard to your own presentation, conduct and standard of dress will affect the way they respond to you as a teacher. You should try to wear appropriate clothing, perhaps a track suit or at least suitable trousers, but should always wear appropriate footwear or have bare feet. Body language gives important messages – if you feel or look bored or unenthusiastic, this will make children feel the same way about your lesson. What do you do with your hands? Hands in pockets or arms folded give the wrong messages. Use your arms to gesture, describe, etc.

Your voice is an important 'tool of the trade'. Pitch, volume, tone, vocabulary, stress and phrasing are all important. You will probably need to project your voice more in a physical education teaching space than in your usual classroom.

It can be difficult to assess your own effectiveness with a group of children so discuss your 'lesson delivery' with a colleague who has observed your teaching. Ask for an honest and objective opinion about whether your instructions were succinct, clear, understood and audible and to what degree you conveyed interest and enthusiasm.

Aim to develop a good teacher/child relationship that raises children's self-esteem and self-discipline alongside an awareness of their own limitations. A poorly considered comment can have a devastating effect on a child's self-esteem.

Use of Demonstration

Demonstration by you or by individuals or groups in the class can be an invaluable teaching aid. Relating demonstrations to your teaching objective helps the children focus on the teaching and learning objective of the lesson. Demonstration can be used to show children:

how to set up equipment
imaginative ideas
a range of responses to task set
the mastery of a skill
improvement
cooperation.

It is important to ensure that during a demonstration, all the children can see and are sitting out of the way of the apparatus and any moving children. You may 'talk' through certain points if this is helpful and not distracting. Give the children who are observing something specific to watch out for, to focus on, thus encouraging them in their ability to observe closely, make judgements and comment positively upon the work of others. You might choose to have more than one child demonstrating a similar point at the same time. Sometimes it is necessary to repeat an action several times in order to make a specific point clear to everyone.

It can be tempting to choose the physically most able children to show their work but this can make other children feel inadequate or it may make a child tackle a difficult skill that is beyond the level of his/her ability. Always check first that children are willing to 'show' their work and are clear about what it is you want them to demonstrate.

It is important to follow up a demonstration with a further 'try' for the whole class and/or a discussion about the points observed. It is tempting to conclude the lesson with a demonstration as the whole class will probably be seated and quiet, but this would not give them an opportunity to apply the purpose of the demonstration in their own work. Also finishing with a demonstration can make the rest of the class feel that their own work has not been valued by the teacher. (See Study Sheet 14.)

Safety

Points of Safety Related to Management and Organization

Teachers must make safety a priority without stifling the adventurous spirit of children. All lessons carry some degree of risk and you must show in your planning and teaching that you have considered all the safety issues related to each lesson and that you help children to develop their own ability to manage risk and be aware of their own safety and that of others.

Ensure that children change in a calm and quiet manner. Do they know what to do when they are ready? How will you move them to and from the teaching space? Leading a line of children from the front through the school is not a good idea, as the children at the back can be a long way from you!

In order for children to have confidence in your ability to organize and teach, you need to establish yourself as the 'one who is in charge'. From the very beginning you need to carefully select and establish clear starting and stopping signals and expect a quick response to them. It is most important that the children respect you and your authority. A whistle is useful if working in a large area outdoors, but should not be used indoors unless an emergency occurs. A quiet working atmosphere enables a teacher to immediately hear and see if problems are arising, and also enables children to respond quickly to a command to 'Stop working please' or 'Freeze'.

In your planning, set tasks that are suitable for your teaching space. You will need to consider space, temperature and weather, the number and size of the children and the equipment/apparatus you want to use. Avoid situations in which children become over-fatigued, take too great a risk or have sole responsibility for the safety of others. Beware of asking children to tackle tasks beyond their level of confidence, and discourage public displays of daring and bravado.

All schools have a Health and Safety Policy – make sure that you read and understand it. In the event of an accident, stop the children from working whilst you deal with the injured child and send two sensible children to obtain help. Never leave your class of children unattended. Make sure that you know where the nearest first aid equipment is kept and who are the qualified first aiders. A basic knowledge of preliminary first aid measures is very useful.

Points of Safety Related to the Working Environment

Although safety is **your** responsibility, you also have a responsibility to train the children to be safety conscious.

You need to ensure that physical education equipment is well maintained. It is usually inspected yearly by an outside agency, but if you spot a potential problem, report it to the subject leader or headteacher. Make sure the equipment children are using is appropriate for the task and for the abilities of the children. The size, condition, weight, composition of materials and apparatus layout are all likely to affect performance.

You should make sure that the floor or outdoor surface is safe for the activities you are setting. Indoors, be aware of substances on the floor, especially after lunch! Outside, be aware of fallen leaves and areas with gravel.

It is important to encourage children to be aware of the potential hazards of such things as radiators, tables, pianos, windows, etc. Remove excess equipment from the working area when possible before the lesson or at least push the piano flat against the side of the hall and stack any spare chairs. Make sure that physical education apparatus is placed in the safest space for the expected task. Remember not to send an entire class of children to fetch equipment from one place at once. Have the equipment spread around and/or send the class in groups.

Glare from bright sunshine can hamper vision so when you are talking to the whole class, make sure that where possible no-one is facing into the sun. You may need to close some curtains or lower blinds.

Points of Safety Related to Health and Fitness

Be aware of those children in the class who may have a medical, physical, social, emotional or behavioural problem that could affect their performance, safety or health during physical education lessons. You may need to bear these children in mind during the planning stage. You are not expected to know details about every medical condition that might affect a child in your class, but if a child in your class is epileptic or diabetic for instance, then it is your responsibility to become informed about their condition. Look at their records, speak to other teachers, their parents and, of course, the child.

You must ensure that you enforce the school's physical education policy on suitable dress and footwear as well as policies about jewellery, hair and wearing glasses. Although it is your responsibility to ensure that children are suitably dressed, make the children aware of the dangers, for themselves and others, of jewellery, long hair and inappropriate or loose clothing or footwear. Continually check for loose shoe laces!

Encourage children in their awareness of how they use the working space, equipment and apparatus so as not to endanger themselves or others. The National Curriculum states that children should be taught to adopt the best possible posture and how to lift, carry and place equipment safely. Use every opportunity to do this during your lessons.

You must provide warm-up time during lessons in order to prepare the muscles, joints and the respiratory system before activity and also time at the end to recover. Ensure that the children begin to appreciate the need for this as part of their own understanding of health and fitness. Set specific warm-up activities that relate to the body parts that will be used most extensively during the lesson.

Points of Safety Relating to Planning and Preparation

Your lessons should provide a balanced experience suitable for the age, physical, intellectual, emotional and social development of the group of children, and also appropriate for the working area and equipment available. Remember every child has the right to experience challenge, success and enjoyment through their physical education programme, so select and set tasks that are appropriate to the children's stage of development, their ability and their level of understanding and cooperation. Open-ended tasks that allow for differentiated outcomes or tasks that are themselves differentiated should be used.

Good lessons aim for maximum participation for all children for the maximum amount of time. You should try to minimize the time that children spend queuing, sitting listening to instructions, and not being actively involved in the lesson. If children become bored through inactivity, they will probably create their own forms of amusement and distraction!

Aim to have all the equipment readily available before the lesson. Grouping children beforehand is also helpful and allows more time to be spent on the lesson itself.

Whilst you are relatively inexperienced, you may wish to have your lesson plans available. Do not hold them whilst teaching but put them at the side of the room. Notes on a postcard in your pocket offer helpful but discrete reminders if you are worried about remembering what you plan to do.

Physical education activities can contribute a great deal to children's entitlement to a broad, balanced curriculum but they also carry a degree of risk. Drinking a cup of hot coffee or getting out of bed in the morning also carry elements of risk but we all do both things regularly with not too much ill effect. Safety cannot be guaranteed but with an awareness of the risks involved and good planning and good management then the risks will be minimized (see Study Sheets 12 and 15).

Physical Education and Children with Special Needs in the Mainstream Class

In all classes there are some children with particular educational needs resulting from behavioural, emotional, physical or learning difficulties. There may also be some children of exceptional ability – particularly in physical education. In aiming to provide a balanced curriculum for all, teachers will need to adapt aspects of their teaching in order to challenge and involve children with specific difficulties or specific talents.

Different special needs will present different problems for the child and for the teacher. Some children will experience difficulties in physical education lessons but nowhere else within the curriculum, whilst others may have serious learning difficulties in the classroom but are capable of high achievement in physical activities. Very able and experienced children may well know a great deal more about Olympic Gymnastics or competitive football than their teacher! The needs of children in this category may be met by recognizing that other aspects of the physical education programme can offer them new experiences.

Understanding each child's strengths and weaknesses will be the best resource in planning appropriate work. No child should be expected to participate in activities that could aggravate their difficulties or expose them to public embarrassment or failure. Alongside this must be a philosophy that reflects the belief in the right of all children to participate actively in physical education lessons at a level appropriate to individual capabilities and to experience challenge and success. As long as a child is not hurt physically, emotionally or socially, then the physical education lesson can be a means of providing very fulfilling and profitable experiences for all children with special education needs.

Access to the Curriculum

The areas of activity for each key stage should be taught to the great majority of pupils in the key stage in ways appropriate to their abilities. For a small number of pupils, material may be selected from earlier or later key stages where this is necessary to enable individual pupils to progress and demonstrate achievement. It is important to present such material in contexts suitable to the pupil's age. Appropriate provision should be made for pupils who need to use:

- means of communication other than speech, including computers, technological aids, signing, symbols or lip-reading
- non-sighted methods of reading, such as Braille, or non-visual or non-aural ways of acquiring information
- technological aids in practical and written work
- aids or adapted equipment to allow access to practical activities within and beyond school.

Appropriate provision should be made for those pupils who need activities to be adapted in order to participate in physical education.

Judgements made in relation to the end of key stage descriptions should allow for the provision above, where appropriate.

(Taken from *Physical Education in the National Curriculum*,
DFE, 1995, 'Common Requirements')

Adaptation Strategies for Children with Special Needs in Physical Education

It is impossible to provide specific guidelines for every situation that teachers are likely to encounter. Therefore it is necessary to give general guidance about some of the available alternatives. The following suggestions are mainly intended for children with some area of difficulty rather than those with special skill or expertise. Individual situations and specific areas of the physical education curriculum will all make different demands upon the commitment and ingenuity of teachers. Without such a commitment children may be denied full access to an enjoyable and meaningful physical education programme. Being able to provide an appropriate physical education curriculum for pupils with special needs depends on a wide range of adaptation strategies.

Individual children's needs should be considered at the planning stage. Adaptation of activities and equipment may be required as well as adaptation to tasks set or the rules of a game. Sometimes the usual technical skills required to play a game can be substituted by skills that a particular child can do with some degree of confidence. Equipment may be modified but try to use unadapted equipment whenever possible. It is most important to work closely with the child, support staff and where possible, involve them in the planning process.

Aim to plan physical education lessons to include rather than exclude. For example, a non-mobile child can roll (send) a ball by:

rolling it down the body from a seated position
rolling it using a gutter or tube.

A non-mobile child can gather (receive) a ball by:

stopping it with any part of the body
stopping it with part of the wheelchair, frame, etc.
having the ball (quoit or 'koosh' ball) tied to a string and then retrieving it.

Generally, do not underestimate the ability of disabled children. Talk with them and find out what they can do – they are often very creative about adaptations. The handbook 'Including Young Disabled People', which supports the 'TOP Play and BT TOP Sport' games materials (Youth Sport Trust, 1996) is a very useful resource for adapting games at Key Stages 1 and 2. Also available is 'TOPS Ability', a training course with accompanying equipment and information cards, which offer advice about the inclusion of disabled children in games activities. Contact your local physical education advisor for further information.

Adaptation of Expectation

Some children may experience difficulty with changing their clothes for physical education. Teachers may need to plan for extra time for these children so that they are enabled to be as independent as possible when dressing and undressing. Often wearing a variation of the suggested school physical education kit, which is easier to put on and take off, can increase a child's independence. Some children get cold very quickly, some asthmatic children find exercising on very cold days can cause difficulties and some children are very vulnerable to physical contact. Whatever children's needs may be, with prior consideration and careful planning, most needs can be met and expectations adapted. All children will achieve at different levels in the different activity areas of physical education and children with special needs are not different in this respect.

Adaptation of Grouping

In some circumstances, it can be useful for everyone when able and less able children work together. In 'over-the-net'-type games activities, a poor sender creates a challenge for an able partner who is then more likely to be able to return the ball to his/her partner sympathetically so that it can be returned again. In other contexts it may be more appropriate to group children according to their developmental or ability level. However, there are emotional and social needs to be met through physical education and always working in a 'special group' can do more harm than good for some children.

Management issues to consider when working with children with mobility problems

- When drawing together the whole class, try to group the class close to the child with impaired mobility rather than at the other end of the hall or field.
- If the rest of the class are standing, make sure that a seated child can see you.

Management issues to consider when working with visually impaired children

- Most visually impaired children have some sight, although the degree and extent of vision varies. Find out what works best for each child. Some light conditions are more appropriate and some particular colours can make quite a difference to the child.
- Use the child's name to attract their attention. Provide verbal information that is specific and accurate – an imaginary clock face can help with locating objects or targets.
- Use balls with integral bells if these help with location. Ensure that the child is given the opportunity to feel where objects are located.

Management issues to consider when working with hearing-impaired children

- Stand still when speaking and face the child when possible.

■ Allow the child to wear hearing aids or devices at the beginning of the lesson when you could outline the general aims of the session. Then they can remove their aids before the practical part of the lesson if necessary.
■ Use a board or demonstration to support your explanations.

With consideration of how children with special needs might access the curriculum being offered, through discussion, careful planning, adaptation of activities and equipment and in some cases one to one support during physical education, they should be challenged, make progress and achieve success and enjoyment in physical education.

Chapter 6

Assessment, Recording and Reporting in
Physical Education

In physical education, children develop their knowledge, understanding and
skills through participating in up to six of the areas of activity and each area of
activity should require them to plan, perform and evaluate their work as well
as achieve, where possible, the expectations laid out in the QCA document
'Maintaining breadth and balance'.

Expectations in Physical Education at Key Stages 1 and 2

The QCA document *Maintaining Breadth and Balance* (1998) identifies what
most children should be able to do in physical education at the end of Key
Stages 1 and 2.

By the end of key stage 1 it is expected that most children will be able to:

In dance

- show control and co-ordination in the basic actions of travelling, jumping,
  turning, gesture and stillness;
- perform simple rhythmic patterns and use movement expressively to explore
  moods and feelings in response to stimuli including music.

In games

- send, receive travel with a ball and similar equipment;
- play simple games that involve running, chasing, dodging and avoiding individually, in pairs and in small groups.

In gymnastic activities

■ perform the basic actions of travelling, rolling, jumping, balancing, climbing and swinging using the floor and apparatus;
■ link actions together both on the floor and using apparatus.

(QCA, 1998)

By the end of key stage 2 it is expected that most children will be able to:

In dance

■ compose and combine basic actions by varying shape, size, direction, level, speed, tension and continuity;
■ express feelings, moods and ideas through movement in response to stimuli including music;
■ perform dances from different times and places.

In games

■ send, receive and travel with a ball with increasing control and accuracy;
■ play individual and simplified small-sided versions of team games;
■ understand and apply the principles of attack and defence.

In gymnastic activities

■ perform different ways of jumping, rolling, turning and balancing, travelling on hands and feet, and climbing and swinging emphasising changes of shape, speed and direction;
■ plan and perform more complex sequences both on the floor and apparatus.

In athletic activities

■ compare and improve their performance and techniques in running, jumping and throwing.

In outdoor and adventurous activities

■ perform activities of a physical and problem-solving nature.

(QCA 1998)

The expectations for swimming are set out differently. Swimming remains a statutory requirement at Key Stage 2 and schools should teach according to the programme of study set out in the National Curriculum Order for physical education. This states that children should be taught:

■ to swim unaided, competently and safely, for at least 25 metres;
■ to develop confidence in water, and how to rest, float and adopt support positions;
■ a variety of means of propulsion using either arms or legs or both, and how to develop effective and efficient swimming strokes on the front and the back;

■ the principles and skills of water safety and survival.

(DFE 1995)

Whilst the QCA expectations are useful, it is important to consider why teachers need to assess in physical education.

What are the Purposes of Assessment?

The purposes of assessment are to:

give appropriate feedback to children
identify progressive learning objectives
provide clear and realistic targets for individual children
establish what pupils know, understand and can do
identify individual pupil needs
motivate pupils
evaluate teaching styles
inform curriculum review and evaluation
reaffirm and communicate priority curriculum aims
improve curriculum planning across the whole school
provide information for other teachers
provide relevant information for parents
provide information for governors
give quality assurance.

Planning and Assessment

Planning and assessment are integral to successful teaching and both planning and assessment can be broken down into the long, medium and short terms.

Assessment in long-term planning will focus on the 'Expectations' and take into account the key learning objectives in the long-term plans for the age group. These assessments will also focus on individuals' achievements and will inform other teachers, parents and the child. Assessment of long-term plans will also inform curriculum review, highlight overall achievement and lead to the setting of future targets for the whole school. This would most often be the responsibility of the physical education subject leader although all teachers will usually be expected to contribute.

Assessment in medium-term planning may take place at the end of a half term or unit of work. These assessments will also be used to record individuals' achievements and to inform curriculum planning but this is likely to be done by each class teacher and will inform their planning for their own class for the next half term.

Short-term planning is for individual lessons and the learning objectives in the lesson plans should be the focus for assessment. As a teacher, you need to demonstrate how well these objectives have been achieved and use this assessment to improve specific aspects of teaching and learning. Assessment of the teaching and learning objectives for individual lessons also form the basis for giving feedback to children during the lesson. Assessment of individual lessons would also inform future planning for children needing additional support or more challenging tasks.

Observation and Assessment

The assessments that relate directly to the teaching and learning objectives for each lesson rely largely on the observational skills of the teacher. Unfortunately, it is not possible to take work from physical education home to mark and assess in your own time. You need to keep your teaching and learning objectives in mind during the lesson as you observe, analyse and assess the children's responses as they plan, perform and evaluate their work. However, you should not only assess through observation. Talking to children and listening to their discussions as they work can provide useful information.

In physical education, observation and assessment go hand in hand. You need to have the skills to observe individual or small groups of children in the midst of a whole class working in a practical way. This is a very challenging task but a useful strategy is to focus particularly on a small group of children for assessment purposes, and rotate the focus over a series of lessons (see Study Sheets 16 and 17).

Recording

It is essential that anything that has been recorded is useful to inform future planning or to inform parents and/or subsequent teachers on the progress of the children. Each school will have a method of recording and as a member of staff you will need to record in line with the policy of your own school. What is recorded should usually relate to teaching and learning objectives and the 'Expectations' for the end of the key stage. Recording systems must be easy to use and efficient, in order to be effective.

Continuum lines can be a useful method of recording children's achievements. Table 6.1 is an example for dance, but this method can be readily adapted for any area of activity with the statements relating to the teaching and learning objectives of the individual lesson, unit of work, or even whole key stage.

Teachers are not able or expected to record all the evidence in every lesson. Focusing on assessing and recording the achievements of a small number of children in each lesson can be a useful and effective strategy, as can using the last lesson of a unit of work as a time to concentrate on assessment and recording. It is important that children learn to make simple judgements about their own performance and that of others and it is possible to use a number of methods of recording, directly involving the children themselves. Examples of possible self-assessment sheets can be found in the following example of the evaluation of gymnastics and in Table 6.2 and Figures 6.1 and 6.2.

Evaluate Your Gymnastics
1   What do you enjoy most in gymnastics lessons?
2   What do you do very well in gymnastics?
3   What do you need to practise?
4   Do you like working on your own? Why?
5   Do you like working with a partner? Why?
6   Do you like working in a group? Why?

TABLE 6.1 Assessment in dance

Observe two/three children during a dance lesson. Mark the continuum lines with their initials to record your assessments of each child's performance. Older children may use a similar system when observing their peers.

Negative		Positive
Moving the feet only	_____	Moving with a change of weights using a variety of body parts
Dances with little structure	_____	Dances with clear beginnings, middles and ends
Moving at the same level	_____	Moving at a variety of changing levels
Moving at the same speed	_____	Moving at a variety of speeds with acceleration and deceleration
Moving in an uninteresting way	_____	Moving showing a variety of ideas
Lack of awareness of what other body parts are doing	_____	Good body shape whilst moving and whilst still
Moving clumsily	_____	Moving sensitively in relation to the floor space and to other children
Little expression of moods/feelings in response to stimulus	_____	Greater expression of moods/feelings in response to stimulus
Little control of body tension, balance and stillness	_____	Developing control of body tension, balance and stillness
Poor rhythmic responses	_____	Developing rhythmic responses

©RoutledgeFalmer

TABLE 6.2   Developing movement vocabulary in gymnastics: learning about body shape

Recording body shapes
Use this chart to draw or write your own record of the body shapes you know

	Balancing	Jumping	Inverting
Small Flexed Tucked			
Straight Long Extended			
Wide Star			

©RoutledgeFalmer

Reporting

Teachers are required by law to report to parents formally once a year and should be familiar with the statutory assessment and reporting requirements. Within physical education teachers need to report on the activities experienced by the children and using teacher assessments and the expectations for each key stage, write a report summing up the achievements of each child.

Ensuring that assessment permeates teaching is not always easy, but with careful long-, medium- and short-term planning, assessment is an essential and effective tool with which to improve achievement and needs to become an integral part of everyday practice for all who teach physical education.

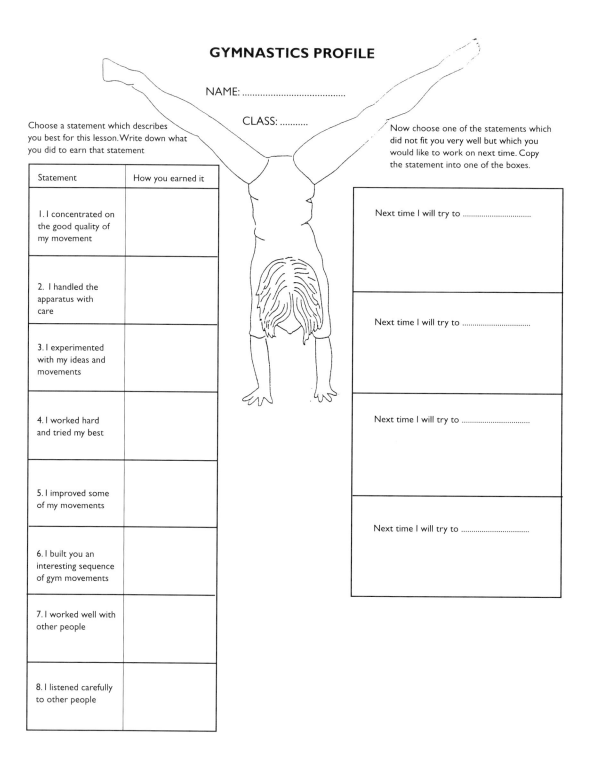

GYMNASTICS PROFILE

NAME: ....

CLASS: ....

Choose a statement which describes you best for this lesson. Write down what you did to earn that statement

Now choose one of the statements which did not fit you very well but which you would like to work on next time. Copy the statement into one of the boxes.

Statement	How you earned it
1. I concentrated on the good quality of my movement	
2. I handled the apparatus with care	
3. I experimented with my ideas and movements	
4. I worked hard and tried my best	
5. I improved some of my movements	
6. I built you an interesting sequence of gym movements	
7. I worked well with other people	
8. I listened carefully to other people	

Next time I will try to ....

Next time I will try to ....

Next time I will try to ....

Next time I will try to ....

FIGURE 6.1   Gymnastics profile

©RoutledgeFalmer

Working with my knees, ankles and toes

body part	very good work	good work	needs practice
straight knees			
straight ankles			
pointed toes			
knees, ankles and toes beautifully controlled			

FIGURE 6.2   Working with my knees, ankles and toes

©RoutledgeFalmer

Chapter 7 Study Sheets

The following sheets can be used by teachers to develop their own expertise, with subject leaders working alongside their colleagues or trainee teachers.

Categories of Games Skills

Games skills can be categorized into three areas: 'sending', 'receiving' or 'travelling with'.

Following either practical experience or observation of games teaching, list (or draw) the activities in the appropriate category. Some activities may need to be put in more than one category.

Sending	Receiving	Travelling with

e.g. push a large ball
with your foot

Observing Playtimes

Observing children at playtime can tell you a great deal about their levels of activity, motor development and fitness.

Make notes on the children's physical activities

Which aspects of their playtime activities feed into games?

Differentiation in Games Activities

All individual, paired or small-group activities can be differentiated in order to suit the children's needs. Differentiation strategies might include adapting equipment, space, being still or on the move, groupings or the requirements of the task.

Outline of Activity
(draw and/or write)

Differentiation Possibilities

Games Skills Progression

No skill is simple until you can do it! Choose a basic games skill (e.g. throwing, catching, kicking, etc.). Track how you might develop this skill from Reception through to Year 6 by showing a progressive list of appropriate individual, paired and small-group activities.

Skill of: _____   **Skill of:** _____

Reception

Year 2

Years 3–4

Years 5–6

Analysis of Games Skills – Sending and Receiving

Consider the preparation, action and recovery phase of the skills of rolling, catching with two hands, hitting a ball with a bat and throwing a small ball overarm.

Record possible teaching points (what you might say to a child to help them be more successful) for each phase of each skill.

Remember to think about the whole body and not just the hands.

Rolling

Possible teaching points at each phase of the action

Preparation	
Action	
Recovery	

Catching with two hands

Possible teaching points at each phase of the action

Preparation	
Action	
Recovery	

Hitting a ball with a bat

Possible teaching points at each phase of the action

Preparation	
Action	
Recovery	

Throwing a small ball overarm

Possible teaching points at each phase of the action

Preparation	
Action	
Recovery	

Gymnastics Apparatus   Age of class: _____

Observing a colleague teaching gymnastics can offer new ideas for using apparatus and the opportunity to analyse children's responses.

Quickly draw a labelled diagram showing the layout of the gymnastic apparatus used in the lesson you are observing.

List the skills that the children do at each apparatus set. Try to discuss with the children the movements each set is best suited to for practising.

Observing and Analysing Gymnastic Actions

Analyse what happens to each part of the body during the preparation, the action and the recovery/landing phases of these actions.

	Upward jump from two feet to land on two feet	Forward roll
Preparation		
Action		
Recovery		

Skill Progression in Gymnastics

Use the chart below to record activities which might **precede** and help to develop the named skill and those which might **follow** and challenge the gymnast to develop new movement vocabulary, once the skill is achieved.

Progressions to precede and to help achieve the skill		
Backward roll	Handstand	Cartwheel

Activities to follow and to extend the skill		
Backward roll	Handstand	Cartwheel

Music for Dance

In order to help you to begin to build up your own resources for dance, consider which music from your own collection might be useful. Then begin to investigate other sources – friends, parents, schools, music shops, etc.

Title					
Composer/ Group					
Mood					
Action words					
Main movement ideas					
Possibilities for cross-curricular links					

Cross-curricular Stimuli for Dance

Cross-curricular links can make learning more meaningful for children and can make economical use of time and resources.

Select one aspect of the science, history and language curriculum for your key stage, e.g. materials. Plan how you might develop these into dance by choosing a suitable stimulus, action words and possible music.

	Science	History	Language
Aspect of curriculum	materials (paper)		
Possible stimuli	large pieces of a variety of types of paper, e.g. newspaper, tissue		
Useful action words	scrunching stretching smoothing folding wrapping tearing floating		
Music	'Orinoco Flow' on 'Watermark' by Enya		

Observing Physical Education Lessons

Much can be learned by watching a peer teach physical education. This sheet will help you to focus your observations.

Area of activity: ------------   **Date:** ------------   **Age of class:** ------------

Make notes on:
Safety, organization and management, and the equipment being used

Teaching points offered to the children by the teacher

The intended teaching and learning objectives

Observation, Evaluation and Evidence Gathering

To help further develop your observation skills, ability to evaluate and gain evidence, make notes on the following, either after observing another teacher teach a physical education lesson or after teaching a lesson yourself.

1 Safety, organization and management of children, equipment, space and time.

2 Session content, appropriateness of tasks for the abilities and experience of individual pupils and the group/class.

3 Provision of feedback. Appropriateness of teaching points to the children's progress in learning.

4 Achievement of teaching and learning objectives. How far were objectives achieved? If not, why not? What next?

5 What have you learned about teaching physical education from this experience?

When Observing a Peer or Reflecting on Your Own Physical Education Teaching Consider:

Warm-up:

■ Were all parts of the body warmed up?

■ Did the children become a little 'out of breath'?

■ Were the spatial boundaries for the children clearly identified?

■ Did the children experience the whole of the available working space during the warm-up?

Development:

■ Were instructions clearly given?

■ Were all the children listening and able to hear?

■ Did any of the activities take a long time to organize and set up? If so, how could this be improved?

■ Were the children physically active for most of the lesson?

■ Were appropriate demonstrations used to aid understanding?

■ Were appropriate teaching points given to help the children improve their performance? Record some examples of teaching points given.

■ Was there evidence of differentiation? Record examples of differentiation.

■ Was the equipment used appropriately? Can you make some constructive comments?

■ Were the children working as safely as possible? List some positive and negative examples of 'safety'.

Child Observation in Physical Education Lessons (1)

Area of activity: ------------   **Date:** ------------   **Age of class:** ------------

Much can be learned about physical education teaching and learning by focusing on two or three children during a lesson. This is most effective when you are observing a colleague teaching, but can also be done when you are responsible for the class.

Observe two/three children closely. Consider the differences in their motor development and their responses to the tasks set.

Child 1   Child 2   Child 3

Child Observation in Physical Education Lessons (2)

Much can be learned about physical education teaching and learning by focusing on two or three children during a lesson. This is most effective when you are observing a colleague teaching, but can also be done when you are responsible for the class.

Area of PoS: ------------   **Date:** ------------   **Age of class:** ------------

Observe two contrasting children closely.
Identify the tasks set

Consider their understanding of the tasks

Consider the quality and range of movement performed

What have the children learnt during the lesson?

Appendix A: Expectations of Trainee Teachers' Work with Children in Primary Physical Education

This sheet is included mainly as a guide for trainee teachers and their school mentors, but inexperienced teachers may also find it useful.

1   A qualified teacher should always be in attendance throughout each session to take overall responsibility for the safety of the children.
2   The trainee teacher should have clear lesson plans indicating:

■ the teaching and learning objectives for the lesson
■ details of the class and the equipment/ apparatus required
■ a series of progressive activities
■ teaching points (feedback) as appropriate
■ organizational and safety points
■ the assessment focus, related to the teaching and learning objective.

3   The lesson will often be in four sections as follows:

■ introductory warming-up activities
■ a progressive series of activities that should develop the teaching and learning objectives and include skill development
■ a main activity – small-sided games playing, composing dance, apparatus experience, depending on the area of activity
■ concluding activities – cool-down, sharing of ideas and experiences.

4   A good trainee teacher will lead a lesson that offers:

- a well-organized environment that maximizes children's safety
- maximum participation for each child with no queuing, teacher talk mini-mized, much individual activity and some group work
- a quiet working atmosphere with encouragement for all children
- progressive activities to improve children's technical skill and quality of performance
- many teaching points offered one or two at a time to extend children's learning and understanding
- demonstrations by children or trainee teacher to provide opportunities to learn from observation and make simple judgements
- questioning, to develop children's movement vocabulary, observational skills and use of language
- appropriate organization of children, time and equipment
- cross-curricular links as appropriate
- integration of health-related exercise
- opportunities for children to plan, perform and evaluate their work
- above all, exercise, success, learning, encouragement and enjoyment for each child.

5   A good trainee teacher will:

- be in a position to observe all the children throughout the session
- give brief, succinct, clear explanations and instructions that the children can hear and understand
- make appropriate use of voice, gesture and demonstration, to motivate and enthuse children
- respond to children's movements and begin to teach from observation using appropriate teaching points
- demonstrate sound knowledge of the current requirements for physical education at Key Stage 1 or 2.

Appendix B: Blank Lesson Plan

TABLE A.1   An example of a lesson plan for Key Stage 1 or 2

Area of activity: *Unit of work*:

Teaching and learning objectives: *Assessment focus*:

Date: *Class*:   *Age*:   *No. of children*:

Lesson structure and timing	Progressive activities
Warm-up	
Development	
Conclusion/Cool-down	

©RoutledgeFalmer

Lesson number:

Duration:	*Venue:*	*Resources: (Use overleaf for plan of apparatus layout)*
Differentiation possibilities	*Teaching points and feedback*	*Management and safety*

References and Further Reading

General

BOARD OF EDUCATION (1933) *Syllabus of Physical Training for Schools*, London: HMSO.

BRITISH ASSOCIATION OF ADVISORS AND LECTURERS IN PHYSICAL EDUCATION (BAALPE) (1995) *Safe Practice in Physical Education*, Dudley: Dudley LEA.

DEPARTMENT FOR EDUCATION (DFE) (1995) *Physical Education in the National Curriculum*, London: HMSO.

HEATH, W., GREGORY, C., MONEY, J., PEAT, G., SMITH, J. and STRATTON, G. (1994) *Blue Prints: Physical Education Key Stage 1*, Cheltenham: Stanley Thomas.

—— (1995) *Blue Prints: Physical Education Key Stage 2*, Cheltenham: Stanley Thomas.

HMSO (1953) *Planning the Programme: Physical Education in the Primary School*, London: HMSO.

MANNERS, H.K. and CARROLL, M.E. (1995) *A Framework for Physical Education in the Early Years*, London: Falmer Press.

PAIN, S., PRICE, L., FOREST-JONES, G. and LONGHURST, J. (1997) *Find a Space*, London: David Fulton Publishers.

PHYSICAL EDUCATION ASSOCIATION, UK (1995) *Teaching Physical Education at Key Stages 1 and 2*, London: PEA.

QUALIFICATIONS AND CURRICULUM AUTHORITY (QCA) (1998) *Maintaining Breadth and Balance at Key Stages 1 and 2*, London: QCA.

RAYMOND, C. (1998) *Coordinating Physical Education across the Primary School*, London: Falmer Press.

SCHOOL COUNCIL AND ASSESSMENT AUTHORITY (SCAA) (1997) *Expectations in Physical Education at Key Stages 1 and 2*, London: SCAA.

—— (1997) *Teacher Assessment in Key Stage 2*, London: SCAA.

WILLIAMS, A. (ed.) (1989) *Issues in Physical Education for the Primary Years*, London: Falmer Press.

YOUTH SPORT TRUST (1996–2000) *Top Play, BT Top, Sport and Other Primary PE Materials*, Loughborough: Youth Sport Trust.

Games

COOPER, A. (1995) *Starting Games Skills*, Cheltenham: Stanley Thomas.

DEPARTMENT OF NATIONAL HERITAGE (1995) *Sport: Raising the Game*, London: HMSO.

HALL, J. (1995) *Games for Juniors*, London: A & C Black.

READ, B. and EDWARDS, P. (1992) *Teaching Children to Play Games*, Leeds: White Line Publishing Services.

SLEAP, M. (ed.) (1991) *Mini Sport*, Oxford: Heinemann Educational.

Gymnastics

BENN, T. (1994) *Primary Gymnastics*, Cambridge: Cambridge University Press.

CARROLL, M.E. and GARNER, D.R. (1991) *Gymnastics 7–11*, London: Falmer Press.

HALL, J. (1995) *Gymnastics for Juniors*, London: A & C Black.

—— (1996) *Gymnastic Activities for Infants*, London: A & C Black.

MANNERS, H.K. and CARROLL, M.E. (1991) *Gymnastics 4–7*, London: Falmer Press.

MAUDE, P. (1997) *Gymnastics*, London: Hodder & Stoughton.

Dance

EVANS, J. and POWELL, H. (1994) *Inspirations for Dance and Movement*, Leamington Spa: Scholastic Publications.

HALL, J. (1997) *Dance for Infants*, London: A & C Black.

HARRISON, K. (1986) *Look! Look! What I can do!* London: BBC.

—— (1993) *Let's Dance*, London: Hodder & Stoughton.

HARRISON, K. and AUTY, J. (1991) *Dance Ideas*, London: Hodder & Stoughton.

SHREEVES, R. (1990) *Children Dancing*, London: Ward Lock Educational.

—— (1998) *Imaginary Dances*, London: Ward Lock Educational.

UPTON, E. and PAINE, L. (1996) *Up the Sides and Down the Middle*, Devon: Southgate Publishers.

Swimming

ASA (1994) *Swimming: Know the Game*, London: A & C Black.

DAVIES, S. (1992) *Learn Swimming in a Weekend*, Dorling Kindersley.

ELKINGTON, H., CHAMBERLAIN, J. and HATT, R. (1998) *Swimming*, Hodder & Stoughton.

HOGARTH, L. (1998) *Swimming Teaching and Coaching Level 1*, Loughborough: Swimming Times Ltd.

Athletics

O'NEIL, J. (1996) *Athletic Activities for Juniors*, London: A & C Black.

OUTDOOR AND ADVENTUROUS ACTIVITIES

BALAZIK, D. (1995) *Outdoor and Adventurous Activities for Juniors*, London: A & C Black.

GILBERT, M. (1994) *Outdoor Education and Personal Growth*, London: David Fulton Publishers.

MARTIN, B. (1995) *Hunting the Griz*, Nottingham: Davies The Sports People.

McNEILL, C. and RENFREW, T. (1991) *Start Orienteering 6–8, 8–9, 9–10, 7–12 years*, Perthshire: Harvey.

SMITH, A. (1994) *Creative Outdoor Work with Young People*, Lyme Regis: Russell House Publishing Ltd.

STRONG, T. and LEFEVRE, D. (1996) *Parachute Games*, Leeds: Human Kinetics.

HEALTH EDUCATION AND FITNESS

BRAY, S. (1993) *Fitness Fun*, Devon: Southgate Publishers Ltd.

HEALTH EDUCATION AUTHORITY (1989) *Health for Life 1 and 2*, Walton-on-Thames: Nelson.

PAIN, S., PRICE, L., FOREST-JONES, G. and LONGHURST, J. (1997) *Find a Space*, London: David Fulton Publishers.

SLEAP, M. (1995) *The Very Simple Skipping Ideas Book*, Hull: Hull University Press.

OTHERS

JOWSEY, S. (1992) *Can I Play Too!*, London: David Fulton Publishers.

KNIGHT, E. and CHEDZOY, S. (1997) *Physical Education in Primary Schools: Access for All*, London: David Fulton

RUSSELL, J. (1988) *Graded Activities for Children with Motor Difficulties*, Cambridge: Cambridge University Press.

STEWART, D. (1991) *The Right to Movement*, London: Falmer Press.

Index

accidents 63
aiming game 116
aims 100, 135
apparatus, gymnastic *see* gymnastics:
    apparatus; equipment
apparatus layouts *see* gymnastics:
    apparatus
art 93
assessment 40, 48, 58–9, 62, 69, 100,
    104–5, 123, 133–42, 162
athletic activities 5, 7, 87–90, 102–3,
    134, 159; awards schemes 90; cross-
    curricular 92–3; lesson planning 88;
    management 88;
    resources/equipment 88–9; safety
    88–9; skills 87–8; sports days 90;
    teaching points 88; timing and
    measuring 87–9
attack and defence *see* games
awards schemes *see* athletic activities

BAALPE (British Association of
    Advisors and Lecturers in Physical
    Education) 27
back crawl *see* swimming
backward rolls 30, 152
balanced curriculum 102, 104, 128
balancing 4, 5, 28, 29, 31–2, 118–19; *see
    also* gymnastics
basic dance actions *see* dance
basic gymnastic actions *see* gymnastics
behaviour 19, 21, 48, 109, 114, 123,
    127–8
Board of Education 3
body parts 14, 29, 31, 36

body shape 5, 29–30, 34, 36, 37, 49, 53–4
body tension 5, 29, 33, 49, 53, 119
breast stroke *see* swimming

capitation 101
cardiovascular 95, 98
cartwheel 152
catching 12, 19, 20–1, 25, 147, 148; *see
    also* games
categories of games 8–11, 25, 144; *see
    also* games
changing *see* clothing
citizenship 99, 114; *see also* personal
    and social development
climbing 4, 5, 28, 33; *see also* gymnastics
clothing 21, 23, 43, 48, 62–3, 80, 95, 97,
    101, 121, 124–5, 127, 130
cognitive development 11
colour coding 22
community 101–2, 120
competition 4, 14–16, 24–6, 66, 91, 120,
concluding activities 16–18, 42, 57,
    64–7, 88, 98, 105–8, 162
confidence 61, 67, 78, 122, 130
control 11, 48, 62–3, 82, 121–3, 125–6
cool down *see* concluding activities
cooperation 4, 14, 16, 24, 78, 80–1, 91,
    99, 120, 124, 127; *see also* outdoor
    and adventurous activities
creative dance *see* dance
creativity 4, 7, 18, 29, 49–50, 53, 57, 113
cross-curricular links 42, 58, 78, 88,
    92–3, 94, 104, 153–4, 163
cultural development *see* personal and
    social development

health-related fitness/exercise 5, 55,
    92–3, 97–9, 127, 163
hearing impairment *see* special needs
history 15
hitting *see* games: striking and fielding
hopping *see* jumping
humanities 93
hygiene 63, 95, 96

independence *see* personal and social
    development
inexperienced teachers 19, 101, 114, 121,
    123, 128
information and communication
    technology (ICT) 104
instructions 4, 22, 94, 108, 122, 124, 127,
    157, 163
invasion games *see* games

jewellery 101, 127; *see also* clothing
jumping 4–5, 28, 29–30, 34–5, 37, 49,
    87–8, 151; *see also* gymnastics

key skills 10
key stage 1 3–4, 6–7, 17–18, 23, 28, 41,
    48, 61, 63, 95, 102, 106, 116, 133,
    163
key stage 2 3–7, 12, 17–18, 25, 28, 38, 42,
    48, 61, 63, 78, 87, 95, 102–3, 106,
    134, 163
key words 10
kicking 12, 147; *see also* games

landing *see* jumping
language 50, 52, 91, 94, 93, 105, 117,
    154, 163
learning objectives 17–19, 25, 40, 57,
    63–4, 79, 88, 104–5
learning support assistants 102
lesson pace 109, 113
lesson planning 16, 19, 44–8, 57–8,
    79–80, 88–9, 98, 110–11, 121, 126,
    130, 135–6, 162, 164–5; *see also*
    planning
levels 5, 13, 29, 34, 36, 37, 48, 53–4
life-saving *see* swimming
linking actions 4, 14, 24, 28, 35, 37, 39;
    see also gymnastics: sequences
literacy 3, 61, 104
long-term planning 100–4, 135; *see also*
    planning
Loughborough University 27

maintenance 101, 126

Major, J. 7
management 21–3, 42–3, 48, 61–3, 88,
    98, 105, 109, 114, 121, 128, 131,
    155–6, 158, 162,
map work *see* outdoor and adventurous
    activities: orienteering
maturity 11
maximum participation/activity 15, 18,
    90, 98, 114, 127, 163
measuring *see* athletic activities
medical conditions *see* health
medium-term planning 104–5, 135; *see
    also* planning
mobility *see* special needs
mood *see* feelings
motor competence *see* motor
    development
motor development 7, 99, 145, 160; *see
    also* personal and social
    development
movement vocabulary 29, 32, 34–5,
    38–9, 50, 55, 139, 152, 163
music *see* dance

National Curriculum 3, 6, 26, 27, 61, 95,
    104, 127, 129, 134
National Governing Bodies 27
National Literacy Strategy *see* literacy
National Numeracy Strategy *see*
    numeracy
newly qualified teachers *see*
    inexperienced teachers
noise 63, 91, 115, 125, 163
numeracy 3, 61, 104

observation: by children 38–40, 41, 58,
    81, 120, 125; by teacher 18–20, 24–5,
    30, 39, 41, 48, 58, 69, 88, 105, 108,
    119–21, 123–4, 136–7, 144, 145,
    150–1, 155–7, 160–1, 163
organisation *see* management
orienteering *see* outdoor and
    adventurous activities
outdoor and adventurous activities 5–7,
    78–87, 102–3, 134, 159; cooperative
    activities 81–4; cross-curricular
    92–3; map work 85–7; orienteering
    80, 85–7; parachute games 81–3;
    planning 79–87; problem-solving
    activities 80–1; resources/equipment
    78–80; safety 80, 84; trust activities
    84–5
over-the-net type games *see* games